Becoming a

POLICE

OFFICER

A Guide to Successful Entry Level Testing

Larry R. Frerkes

COPPERHOUSE PUBLISHING COMPANY
901-5 Tahoe Blvd.
Incline Village, Nevada 89451
(702) 833-3131 • Fax (702) 833-3133
e-mail info@copperhouse.com
http://www.copperhouse.com/copperhouse

Your Partner in Education
with
"QUALITY BOOKS AT FAIR PRICES"

Becoming a
POLICE OFFICER
A Guide to Successful Entry Level Testing

Library of Congress Catalog Number 98-70933
ISBN 0-942728-88-2 Paper Text Edition

2 3 4 5 6 7 8 9 10

Printed in the United States of America.

DEDICATION

This book is dedicated to my children—Krystal and Larry W., for their love and patience during the many nights of their formative years when I was working the night shift or called out on assignment.

Also to my partner and confidant—Bob Skipworth, who taught me the meaning of true friendship.

PREFACE

You have made a choice to pursue a career in law enforcement. The badge you will wear is symbolic of the commitment you will make to those who will depend on you. Those who wear a badge are marked by it. It sends a message that you embody such personal characteristics as courage, dependability, integrity, strength, and fairness. Affirm your dedication to these principles. Embrace the following excerpt from the *Code of Ethics*:

> I recognize the badge of my office as a symbol of public faith, and I accept it as a public trust to be held so long as I am true to the ethics of the police service.

As you make the transition from private citizen to law enforcement officer, celebrate your achievement with those who matter most— your family. Commitment to family values will empower a successful and rewarding career. Wear the badge with pride. Defend its principles. Emulate the qualities it represents. Treasure it. Keep it polished, gleaming; the reflection of the badge is one of hope, peace and security. Respect your badge and others will too.

Good luck to you always and be safe.

—Larry Frerkes

TABLE OF CONTENTS

Chapter Five
DRUG TESTING 35

Chapter Six
WRITTEN EXAMINATION 39

Chapter Seven
PHYSICAL FITNESS/AGILITY TESTING 53

Chapter Thirteen
THE CHOICE IS MADE 125

Appendix
WHERE AND HOW TO FIND JOB OPENINGS .. 129

Chapter One

UNDERSTANDING THE JOB

Career Preparation

In today's complex society, choosing a career is one of the most important decisions you will make in your life. Ideally, the trick is to find a job that you would do for free if life afforded you the opportunity. To many, a career in law enforcement has such strong appeal that it closely meets this distinction. Police work offers rewards and challenges unequaled in other professions. It can also be demoralizing and laden with stress. As an officer, you will be vulnerable to fierce inclement weather, grueling work hours and life threatening calls for service. Before you put a badge on your chest, invest the time and energy to determine if the law enforcement profession is right for you. You owe it to your friends, loved ones and yourself to make an informed decision. The attrition rate of young officers is a testament of those falsely believing that police work was suited for them. It is not a career for everyone, but for those meant for the job, many would do it for free if they didn't need to collect a paycheck. This concept may be somewhat melodramatic, but it applies to those applicants with passion and ambition who are attracted to the nature of police work.

As you carefully consider all aspects of the job, the law enforcement agency you are considering will also carefully evaluate you and whether you would qualify for their organization. The competition you will encounter is keen. The testing is tough. Police departments have a responsibility to taxpayers to attract only the highest caliber of recruit. Personnel costs are the largest portion of a police budget. Turnover and attrition is costly to every department. It is essential that newly hired officers are motivated, competent and committed to the agency. It doesn't matter whether it's the New York City Police Department with 30,000 officers or a one officer department in Montana, only the best applicant will be selected. For every officer who is hired, there are 250 applicants who are not. The secret to accomplishing your dream comes down to one objective—preparation.

INTERESTED IN BECOMING A SUCCESSFUL POLICE OFFICER CANDIDATE?

You Must:

Prepare
Be Dedicated
Test Effectively
Be Highly Educated
Understand Priorities
Make Informed Decisions
Invest in Your Career Goal
Perform Well Under Pressure
Turn Your Ambition Into Reality
Understand the Selection Process
Be in Excellent Physical Condition
Have Effective Communication Skills
Have Desire for Unlimited Personal Growth
Have Desire for Unlimited Professional Growth

PREPARATION IS INDISPENSIBLE TO SUCCESS!

"Prepare for the day opportunity presents itself, and you will be rewarded."

President Abraham Lincoln

There are far too many aspiring police officers who fail to prepare themselves for the testing process. A recent study conducted by Stanard and Associates provided startling findings in this regard. As one of the largest studies ever conducted to examine the skills and personality characteristics of law enforcement applicants, which included 10,000 applicants over three years, Stanard and Associates acknowledged that the pool from which new police recruits are selected is enormous, but it is of generally poor quality. The study disclosed that many candidates do not possess the basic skills needed to perform the job. Twenty-five percent of the candidates could not read at a twelfth grade level, and 33 percent were not proficient at basic math skills needed to perform essential functions of the job. Six percent of the applicants had illegal drugs in their systems on the day of testing, 40 percent had arrest records, 15 percent had been convicted of a crime, and 20 percent had been fired from a job.

These results indicate a great percentage of applicants are unacceptable and would be rejected at some point in the selection process. They also infer that many of the applicants failed to invest the effort to understand what is required to be hired as a police officer. Preparation is where a successful applicant separates him/herself from the others. When you train and educate yourself, you build personal values, confidence, credibility and self-esteem. Mastering the principles of preparation can turn your energy, enthusiasm and motivation into the success that you covet.

". . .blessed are the meek for they shall inherit the earth. Blessed are those who protect the meek from those who would take the inheritance by violence and force. They shall be called policemen."

Author Unknown

This quote may not define all of what a police officer is asked to do, but it does depict how they are valued by those who depend on their protection. If you ask ten police executives to define the exact nature of the job of a police officer, you very well may receive ten different variations. There is no one simple definition. Certainly, a police officer's job is to protect life and property and enforce all statutes, laws and ordinances. They are to deter, detect, and apprehend miscreants engaged in criminal activity. A police officer collects, assembles, and logs evidence, compiles reports, prepares cases for trial, and testifies on behalf of the state. A thorough definition is almost unlimited.

One element of the job that all law enforcement officials will acknowledge is the potentially fatal risk of wearing a badge. Fatalities in the line of duty are a fact of a life. Despite law enforcement official's best efforts to minimize risk, they will never be able to eliminate the reality of "killed in the line of duty." Society has grown increasingly violent, and it is the officers on the street who are the first line of defense for us all.

Has police manpower managed to keep pace with the rising tide of crime in the last forty years?

No. Police executives are constantly ordered to do more with less. Shrinking budgets result in fewer officers to handle more calls for service. In 1960, there were three police officers for every reported violent crime. In 1990, there was only one officer for every three violent crimes reported.

What is not always enumerated in a job announcement are the not-so-evident expectations, but expectations nonetheless. A police officer is a role model. You may not ask for that title, but it comes with the badge when you choose to put it on. Both your personal and official life must be conducted in an exemplary manner. You are constantly in the lens of the video camera and under the scrutiny of the public microscope. Your actions and conduct in the performance of your duties must not be influenced by personal bias, emotions, or friendships. You cannot walk away from the burden of notifying a parent of the death of a child, or the stench of a urine soaked, feces covered crib of an infant after responding to a report of child abuse. You are required to remain calm in the face of danger, restrain your actions, and constantly concern yourself with the welfare of others at the expense of your own, if necessary.

You must make a commitment to the profession because the work requires long and irregular hours and holiday shifts, which means your current normal social relationships with friends and family will suffer. You must be prepared to accept these restrictions. It is essential that you initiate communication with family members and discuss the disagreeable factors associated with police work. Rarely are these factors mentioned in a job description, but they are just as common as arresting a drunk driver. It comes with the territory. As you reflect upon these thoughts, what you must remember is to keep the job in perspective. It is suggested that you do not live for the job! Rather, the job is there to live. Family must always come first.

When you go before your first police hiring oral board, you might be asked to define the role of a police officer. You may be asked to explain your own motivation to become a police officer. Prepare your thoughts now.

Assignments

One of the most appealing aspects of a career in law enforcement is its variety of work assignments. All occupations recognize the need for reassignments to avoid "burnout." Changing the work site or principal assignment revitalizes staff and enhances productivity. Sick leave and attrition is reduced. Morale rises, and with that comes a positive image of the department projected to the community. You are the police department to those you service in the performance of your duties.

Before you announce to an oral board that you will be the next detective in the homicide unit, or member on the S.W.A.T. team, remember your current level in the system. You are a rookie. As a "rook," you can expect to "do your time" in a "black and white" (patrol unit). The assignment in the Field Services Bureau (patrol division) is the building block and foundation of a successful career in law enforcement. Career goals are healthy, but don't rush it Homicide detectives, tactical unit officers, motorcycle officers, etc. all started in the patrol division. Experience, knowledge, specialized skills, understanding of human behavior and the criminal mind require time. When qualified, an officer may have an opportunity to seek specialized assignments, depending on the size of the agency. These may include:

- Criminal Investigator
- Crime Prevention
- Horse Mounted Patrol
- Traffic Enforcement
- FTO (Field Training Officer)
- School Liaison Officer
- Fixed Wing/Helicopter Unit
- Undercover Narcotics
- Crime Scene Unit
- Tactical Unit (S.W.A.T.)
- Research and Development
- D.A.R.E. Officer
- Street Gang Unit

- Forensics
- Youth Services Bureau
- Training Division
- Bomb Squad
- Hostage Negotiator
- Internal Affairs Unit
- Vice Officer
- Identification
- K-9 Unit
- Motorcycle Patrol
- Intelligence Unit
- Sex Crimes Unit
- Extradition Unit

Geographical Considerations

Have you thought about where you would like to be a police officer? Have you given consideration to your personal and family needs? Do not be so anxious to wear a badge that you would be willing to accept a job offer regardless of where it is. There are consequences to accepting a position, or even testing for a position, in an area that is not suitable or practical for the next 20 years of your life. You should consider the following:

Cost of Testing

Undoubtedly, your desire to find a police department that is hiring, will cause you to "flood" the country with letters of intent. Is it practical to test in all the states you sent letters to? Can you afford to test in all of those departments, particularly if they are out of state? Often, police agencies will accommodate out-of-state applicants by arranging for all of the testing stages in a one- or two-day period. This minimizes your expenses; however, this will not always be the case. You may be required to travel to the agency several times to complete each of the testing phases. For most people, this is cost-prohibitive. If you can't afford to make these trips, then look for suitable agencies and save your money.

Be selective and know in advance what requirements agencies have. You may very well have a particular agency in mind and are willing to spend whatever it takes to work for that agency. More power to you! If that is your goal, then plan accordingly.

Climate

Have you given thought to the weather in the area where you want to apply? This may seem inconsequential at the time of your application, but it can be a real issue. If you have lived in Southern California all of your life, will you enjoy working in snowy conditions four months out of the year in eastern Montana? The same principle may apply if you are accustomed to cool, rainy days along the Oregon coast, and then accept a job in Las Vegas, Nevada, where the heat can be unbearable. Salary, benefits, and advancement opportunities are all important in your decision-making process. But so is the weather.

Law enforcement officers belong to a select group of occupations that require employees to endure the fury of mother nature. Firefighters, ambulance crews, utility repair crews and police officers, among others, must work in conditions that the normal population does not. When governmental agencies, school districts and the private sector shut down due to a severe blizzard, the police officer remains on the beat. Think of the hardship involved in directing traffic in -20 degree weather or sitting on a police motorcycle, with its motor generating its own treacherous heat, in 112 degree weather. If you are looking for a climate friendly environment, you may want to consider other career alternatives.

Shift Work

Police officers do not work 8 A.M. to 5 p.m., Monday through Friday, with weekends off. A new officer is going to be exposed to all three shifts—day, swing, and graveyard. Remember, as a "rookie," weekends off is a fantasy. After you have between five to eight years on the job, and receive a specialized assignment, your work hours may resemble that of the ordinary worker.

Until that time, accustom yourself to unconventional work hours and irregular days off. You will soon learn the phrase, "Tuesday is my Friday!" New officers often fail to fully comprehend this impact on family. Your participation in family activities is going to change. You may have to accept that you will not be home when your children open their presents on Christmas morning or when your friends and family carve up the Thanksgiving turkey.

Police departments have a variety of work schedules. Work hours are often determined by workload, budget concerns, collective bargaining agreements, and seniority. Five 8-hour shifts are most common. You may work four 10-hour shifts. Some departments work a 12-hour, three days on, three days off, shift. You might even be assigned to a power shift comprised of two day shifts, two swing shifts, and one graveyard shift. Your schedule will begin all over again after just two days of rest.

Occupational Stress

Stress is a fact of life. There is stress in every occupation. Some jobs are more intense than others. Police work is certainly a stressful job. It is inevitable. Yet, stress does not have to be a back-breaker in law enforcement. If you understand the full complexity of the profession and prepare yourself, then it is possible to minimize the repercussions. The legion of activities and peculiarities involved in any given 8-hour shift creates stress all by itself. A simplified explanation of the stress involved in police work can be broken down into four categories:

Organizational Stress
Police work is a paramilitary environment. It is analogous to military structure. Terms such as sergeant, lieutenant, captain, major, platoon, unit, and squad are used in both military and police infrastructures. A military maneuver and a police operation have common aspects. Following an order is a fundamental principle. In an emergency situation, lives may be at stake, and there is no tolerance for a subordinate questioning an order. Failure to follow orders in either system is unacceptable and will be dealt with swiftly and harshly. If you are prone to be resistant to following directions, police work is sure to cause you excessive stress.

Internal Surroundings

A thorough sociological and psychological explanation of the internal causes of stress in police work would require chapters, if not volumes, of books. If not careful, police officers tend to form a subculture among themselves. In some jurisdictions, you quickly learn that police officers are not particularly respected or liked by the citizens they serve. An *Us vs. Them* dichotomy may develop. This subculture may encourage an impressionable officer to adopt a "trust only those in blue" mentality. Also associated with this aspect of police mentality is the phrase, *"Code of Secrecy."*

The *Code of Secrecy* is defined as: Lying to protect yourself and other officers associated with you is justified by the bond among fellow officers and the *fear* of outsiders.

As you can see from the definition, the *Code of Secrecy* illustrates the severity of the breakdown of trust on the part of those responsible to carry out the duties to protect and serve the community. Consequently, a sense of isolation sets in. If you lose the respect of the people you have sworn to serve, then you will begin to distrust the public in return. Soon, the only people you associate with are other police officers. Movies, dinners and parties are attended only with your fellow officer and his/her spouse. Such isolation is not healthy. This is a serious source of stress, and one that does not have to develop. Police departments try to recognize this phenomenon by instituting community policing, sensitivity training, encouraging officer involvement in community youth activities and peer counselor programs. You, too, can combat this social stigma. Be aware of its existence. Do not buy into negativity, and, in particular, do not subscribe to the *Code of Secrecy*! Do not lose sight of your commitment to the public and your appetite to help people. Remember the principle for which you have taken an oath; "To Protect and Serve." And always reflect on and remember your reasons for joining the force.

Individual Stress

This topic was reviewed briefly under the discussion of shift work. Police work will affect you and your significant other in many ways. Besides work hours, days off and holidays, your significant other will struggle every day you walk out the front door to go to work knowing that you may not come home that evening. This fear can take a serious toll at home. Also, what you see and do every day can exact a high price from your emotional and personal stability. Every day, you must deal with life's miseries. When a civilian is repulsed by news coverage of drive-by shootings, homicides, innocent victims of drunk drivers or the horror of child abuse, they merely change the channel or turn the page of the newspaper. The police officer cannot walk away from or ignore the visual facts of society's ills. A police officer has a job to do, and that job must get done, but at what cost? Who will be affected? How long will it take before an officer either learns to either deal with these realities or turns to alcohol, drugs, or becomes physically ill, or resigns.?

External Stress

There is no denying that when you respond to a "man with a gun" call, stress will be involved. It is natural, and it is expected. How you deal with this kind of stress is crucial to your well being. Your life, your partner's life, or the victim's life may be at stake if you fail to handle the situation properly. During the long months of police academy training, you will go through countless scenarios and situational training exercises to learn how to handle these crisis calls. Regardless of how frequently or how well you train, the "real thing" will bring out the adrenaline and the onset of stress. Sometimes police work can be summarized as being 98 percent pure boredom, with 2 percent sheer terror. Unexpected danger is part of the job. Never should any activity be viewed as routine. The first time you stop a "routine" speeder and let your guard down, you may become a statistic.

It is suggested is that an applicant give attention to all factors that will affect you now and in the future. Long-term planning is essential to your professional success and personal happiness.

Chapter Two

SALARY AND BENEFITS

Salary

O ne of the more favorable aspects of a career in law enforcement is one that is often underrated—salary. By and large, many young trainees do, in fact, enter into the field for the salary and benefit package. At the same time, it is the nature of the work, and the fulfillment of their dreams, that has enticed them to wear a badge. In fact, it is interesting that many young officers freely admit that they enjoy the work so much that they would "do it for free." This commitment to public service is often symbolized by the recruitment of new hires from the ranks of police reserve units where volunteers engage in various law enforcement functions without compensation. The primary foundation for motivation is supported by a recent study involving a survey of 100 police cadets. The number one motivation for entering a career in law enforcement is the desire to serve the community, help people and the satisfaction found in working with people. This passion, held by so many wanting to enter this field, is a testament to the ideals of its members. Few professions can boast of this kind of inspiration.

There is a cliche, and it is stereotypical to many, that people enter the private work force for money, and those who enter the government work force do so for security. Maybe that is true for some, but not necessarily in the law enforcement profession. In addition to job satisfaction, law enforcement offers a sound compensation package that will normally allow an officer to raise a family, attain the American dream (home ownership) and live a comfortable life-style. One only needs to note that patrol officers can earn approximately $65,000 per year in New York City, and top police command officers there receive at least twice that.

Many agencies have recognized that to attract and retain qualified law enforcement personnel, they must provide equitable compensation. City councils, county commissions, and state legislative bodies

11

have recognized the same needs. Crime control continues to be in the forefront of public interest. Providing an effective police presence is conditional upon adequately funding police agencies and providing a superior wage for officers. It was not that long ago that a police officer's salary was indeed a disgrace. In addition, improvements in salaries, advancement in benefits and working conditions have been effectively implemented through associations, unions, fraternal orders of police, and professional organizations. Collective bargaining agreements, contracts and excellent working relations between government bodies, police executives and rank-and-file association members have all contributed to the growth of this occupation. You will be entering into a field that will provide a myriad of benefits to promote a life-style of security, advancement, compensation and prosperity. Benefits will differ from agency to agency. Therefore, a broad range of the various types of benefits will be addressed.

Salaries will vary greatly depending upon geographical location. Cost-of-living factors will parallel that of entry level salaries. An entry level salary for the San Jose Police Department in California will be significantly higher than the salary received at the Little Rock, Arkansas Police Department. Overall, salaries are higher in larger, urban jurisdictions. In the early 1990s, the median salary of police officers was approximately $32,000 per year. Those in the middle range earned from $24,500 to $41,200. Contemporary base starting salaries for new-hires ranged from $20,000 to $28,000 per year. Top step salaries reached nearly $65,000 per year. Inquire into the salary of the particular agency you are applying to and insure that it is to your approval before you begin the testing process. Clearly, police work can be a very lucrative career, especially when you consider that many agencies only require a high school education. Few occupations can offer this kind of salary with this minimum level of education.

Longevity Pay

After you have been successfully employed for a predetermined number of years, you may receive compensation in the form of longevity pay. In the simplest terms, longevity pay merely rewards employees for their continuous service. These amounts can be based on a percentage of your salary, or a fixed amount that increases with each year served. It may be paid bi-weekly, monthly, twice yearly, or annually.

Educational Incentive Pay

Most departments recognize the value of employees having received their higher education credentials and reward them accordingly. Salaries are increased on a percentage basis. See Chapter Three on the application process for additional information.

Hazardous Duty Pay/Specialized Assignments

Depending on the nature of assignment, your salary may be increased to compensate for the special skill, training or hazard your assignment may require. Sample assignments which may qualify you to receive an increase in salary may include:

- SWAT Team
- Helicopter Patrol
- Fixed Wing Aircraft
- Motorcycle Patrol
- Undercover Assignments
- Narcotics

- Bilingual Officer
- Bomb Squad
- Mounted Patrol
- Investigation
- K-9
- Field Training Officer

Shift Differential Pay

Shift differential pay is compensation afforded to officers assigned to work hours outside of the normal 8A.M. to 5P.M. business day. Shifts, such as swing and graveyard, are included. Range of compensation may be from 2 percent to 5 percent of the base salary for hours worked.

Health and Medical Insurance

A wide variety of comprehensive major medical programs are offered as a part of your employment contract. These benefits may encompass:

- Medical
- Dental
- Cancer policy
- Dismemberment policy
- Chiropractic care

- Life insurance
- Wellness programs
- Disability insurance
- Vision
- Employee assistance program

Depending on the contracts in place, agencies may cover a portion or the entire premium for employees and dependents.

Sick Leave

Sick leave benefits are standard in the employee package. Sick leave credit at the rate of 10 to 15 days per year is average. Sick leave is provided to ensure continued income in the event of illness or injury to the employees or members of their immediate family.

Sick leave incentive programs encourage employees not to use sick leave, with the objective to increase productivity and decrease loss of time due to illness or injury. Each year employees are awarded additional sick leave or a monetary lump sum.

Vacation Leave

As with sick leave, vacation or annual leave is a standard benefit to new employees. New-hires will generally accrue 12 to 15 days annually. Increase in vacation leave is prorated based on the number of years of service. Some collective bargaining agreements have secured liberal benefits of between five to six weeks of annual leave/vacation yearly for line officers.

Keep in mind that considering the complex, dangerous, and stressful aspects of the job, vacation time is well earned and deserved.

Holiday Pay

Most agencies observe between 10 and 12 holidays each year, depending on contractual agreements. Unique collective bargaining agreements have managed to incorporate a variety of additional days which may include birthday, a floating holiday, and a personal holiday.

Uniform Allowance

Some departments will issue uniforms to officers at no cost to the employee. Others will provide a monthly, biannual or annual sum to cover the cost of purchase, replacement and cleaning of all necessary uniforms, duty belts, inclement weather gear, and weapons.

Retirement/Pension

Most departments contribute to their state Public Employee Retirement System (PERS) plan. However, individual private plans are not uncommon. Another unique benefit available to many departments is the Early Police Officer Retirement Program, which is an enhanced retirement plan designed specifically for commissioned police officers. Sworn officer contributions will vary from state to state. Many systems provide for retirement at the age of 50, depending on the number of years of service; generally that figure is 20 to 25 years. Retirement pay for most departments at age 50 is 50 percent of salary at the time of retirement. Additional benefits and/or increases of base retirement benefits correlate with longer service. Oftentimes, retirement benefits will increase 2 percent for each year beyond the minimum years required for retirement.

Worker's Compensation

Officers who are injured in the line of duty, or who incur occupational illness, receive disability pay. Disability pay is based on a percentage of current salary, length of disability and/or medical necessities and the bargaining unit involved. Disability leave or worker's compensation plans available to law enforcement officers include state-funded privatization plans and self-insured programs.

Funeral Leave

In the event of a death of an officer's immediate family member (spouse, parent, guardian, child, sibling, grandparent, grandchild, in-law, step or any other family members), an officer is granted a leave-of-absence with pay. Normally, these hours are deducted from the officer's accrued sick leave. However, some employee contracts have a separate clause allowing up to five working days in the event of such a tragedy which are not deducted from the officer's personal sick leave.

Educational Assistance

On the same principle as educational incentive pay, police administrators support and uphold the concept that a college-educated officer is an investment in the department's future. Assistance is often provided to the officer who expresses an interest in taking college-level courses. The hiring agency may reimburse the cost of tuition, books and required fees for job-related or career development courses. Ordinarily, these courses must be taken through an accredited/approved educational institution and must be relevant to the field of employment.

Military Leave

Law enforcement agencies abide by federal parameters and grant military leave for members of the National Guard or military reserve forces. Fifteen working days are granted yearly, with pay, and are not subject to deduction of vacation time or sick leave.

Chapter Three

APPLICATION PROCESS

The goal of the application process is to advertise and recruit qualified candidates for law enforcement positions. The application process is just one component of the selection process, which includes the application appraisal and written, oral and practical exams. Each phase shares a common purpose—to establish the necessary minimum requirements, and to test the applicants for the knowledge, skills, and abilities needed to perform the duties of the job.

It is essential that the applicant has a clear understanding of all factors involved in the minimum requirements and selection process. Candidates should be aware of the fact that merely meeting the minimum requirements and passing the various testing phases does not guarantee appointment to the position. However, with prudent preparation and follow-through, an applicant can enhance his/her opportunities and successfully achieve his/her goal.

Completing The Application

Carefully review the directions before filling out the application. If the application calls for black ink, use black ink. If it states "print neatly," then do not have your application typed, print it neatly! If the directions do not specify, have it typed, if possible. In lieu of a typewriter, use black ink and print carefully. If you need additional space to accurately answer a question, then attach an 8 1/2" x 11" sheet of paper with the additional information. Number the additional assignments with the same number and section title as the question you are answering. A neatly prepared application will set the stage for a positive first impression. Do not underestimate the importance of properly addressing all the categories of the application. The professionalism and thoroughness of your application can make the difference.

Being thorough must be your primary concern. The minimum requirements (MQ's) and your application will be scrutinized to insure that you meet all requirements for the job. Typically, a personnel analyst will conduct a thorough evaluation and make the decision whether you will proceed to the testing phases. Do not rely on your resume to detail your education and experience. It is essential that you list all of your education, training, experience and applicable personal accomplishments to meet the minimum requirements. You are cautioned not to falsify or exaggerate your credentials. The background investigator's purpose is to verify that the information you supplied on the application and the personal history statement is complete and accurate. You will find the following noted on all applications:

> "All statements made on applications are subject to verification. False statements may be a cause for disqualification or discharge from employment."

If this particular subject has caused you alarm, and there is some hesitation, then you have no business seeking a career as a law enforcement officer. If there is an issue that concerns you, answer truthfully. That issue will be raised in the background investigation, and you will have the opportunity to explain. Whether you will be successful in the background investigation depends entirely on the severity or nature of that issue and the honesty you display.

Closing Date

It is your responsibility to submit your application prior to the date of closing. *Rarely will an agency accept an application once the deadline has expired.* The advertised deadline for requesting applications was set well before the submission deadline in order to provide ample time for applicants to complete and return requested information. If you are mailing your application, mail it at least one week *before* the deadline. No one has control over when the mail is delivered. Having a postmark prior to the deadline does not guarantee on-time delivery.

Because of the volume of applications received for law enforcement openings, it is vital that you return all items completed in a timely manner. Incomplete applications missing required enclosures will normally be rejected.

If you move or change telephone numbers at any time during the process, it is your responsibility to notify the hiring agency of the change. Do so as soon as possible in order to ensure you will be promptly notified of specific testing dates.

It is always good advice to submit your application well in advance of the closing date. If, for reasons beyond your control, you will not be able to mail your application by the deadline, contact the hiring agency and inquire if sending the application by facsimile would be permissible. Another alternative is to send your package by overnight express mail. But, what purpose does it serve to wait until the last minute? Also, in the event of a tie following the testing process, it may be broken according to the date and time the applications were received by the hiring agency.

Enclosures/Attachments

Undoubtedly, your application will include several attachments. It is suggested that you prepare a personal file with the applicable documents in advance to ensure that your application is complete. The below-mentioned items are not all necessary at the time of the application's submission. However, these items will be necessary when the applicant is called in for the background investigation process. Prepare your personal file now so that you are ready to submit the requested items when needed.

Attachments to prepare in advance are:

- *Application Form.* Read the directions carefully. You may be required to have your application notarized. Failure to do so will result in rejection.

- *Residency.* Based on Federal law, employers must receive proof of legal residency. Proof of U.S. residency or a Declaration of Intent, Immigration and Naturalization Service Form, N-405 is required.

- *Social Security Card.* The applicant must have copies of his/ her social security card. Ensure it is legible and easy to read. If your card has been lost or is too worn to be identified, contact the Social Security Administration in your area for a replacement.

- *Fingerprinting.* You will be fingerprinted by the hiring agency prior to appointment. There may be a fee for this procedure. Plan accordingly.

- *Driver's License.* You must have a legal/valid operator's license if you plan to be a law enforcement officer. Have a copy of your operator's license should it be requested at the application stage. Also, you must be insurable for private motor vehicle insurance coverage. There is no deviation from the rules in this regard.

- *Birth Certificate.* Law enforcement officers must be citizens of the United States. You will be required to submit proof of date and place of birth. Oftentimes, a photocopy is acceptable. You may be required to submit an official copy with a raised seal. A hospital copy is normally not accepted. Only an official copy received from the Bureau of Vital Statistics from the state and/or county in which you were born will be acceptable.

- *Photographs.* While this is not often requested, prepare yourself and have a current photo available (less than one year old). Photos are generally requested by the background investigator prior to the initiation of the background investigation.

- *Educational Transcripts.* It would be advantageous for your file to contain certified, official transcripts from higher education that you have attended. *See subsection Education Requirement in this chapter for detailed information.*

- *Unless specifically directed not to,* always submit a personal resume with your application. Ensure that it is current and professional in content and appearance. If you lack the knowledge to prepare your own resume, contact a professional resume service and let them do it for you.

- *Criminal History.* The ideal law enforcement applicant has led an exemplary life-style free of criminal conduct. Prevailing federal statues, and all 50 states, have codified statutes prohibiting the hiring of an individual with a felony conviction. Law enforcement officers carry a firearm as part of their "normal tools of the trade." Ex-felons are banned from possessing a firearm. This precondition is obvious.

There may be situations that may not constitute an automatic rejection. State-to-state variations of criminal statutes, including felonies and misdemeanors are quite diverse. The hiring agency will classify the conviction by its state's statutes. Thus, an applicant's conviction record will not necessarily be a basis for rejection in the selection process. Law enforcement agencies might also take into account any mitigating factors, which *may* include: date of offense; your age at time of the offense; seriousness and nature of the offense; rehabilitation since the offense; diversion vs. conviction of record; probation with an honorable discharge; conviction dismissal, record sealed, restoration of civil rights, etc.

If you are unsure if you will be disqualified, contact the recruitment office, civil service board, or personnel officer and inquire specifically as to your situation and preferably get an answer in writing before you proceed with the testing process. Above all, do not attempt to conceal or falsify any arrest or conviction, as that alone *will* result in automatic rejection. More details about past criminal acts are discussed further in Chapter 12.

Educational Requirements

Law enforcement is no longer considered merely a "job." Instead, being a police officer is a career and a profession. When the multitude of responsibilities are examined (daily tasks, interpersonal contact and decision-making), the position requires you to be articulate, knowledgeable and intelligent. As such, minimum educational requirements have been established. According to a report in the *New York Times,* 23 percent of all police officers today hold a college degree, compared to only 4 percent in 1970. Two- and four-year colleges in all states and the District of Columbia offer classes in criminal justice, police science, law enforcement and corrections. Four-year programs in criminal justice and public administration will help those who hope to rise to executive positions within law enforcement agencies. Courses helpful for a police career are: English, psychology, sociology, socio-psychology, counseling, public relations, business law, chemistry and physics. More and more departments are increasing their educational requirements. Some require a minimum of 60 credits, while others are require an associate of arts degree, customarily with a major in police science or criminal justice. While not widespread, some more progressive police agencies are requiring a bachelor of arts degree as a minimum educational level. Law enforcement will continue to heighten its minimum educational requirements as society recognizes the need to attracts more educated police officers.

Study after study shows that an educated police officer will experience fewer citizen complaints, incidents of police brutality, and unjustified officer-involved shootings. It is recognized in law enforcement agencies across the nation that increasing the level of education of new officers serves as an integral part in providing effective police services as we move into the 21st century. A recent excerpt published in the *Chief of Police* magazine illustrates this point: ". . . respect for the police will not be attained unless the educational level of officers equals or exceeds that of the general population."

Minimum Requirements

The predominant minimum level of educational requirements is the achievement of a high school diploma. Most of the time, agencies will accept the acquisition of a GED certificate in lieu of a high school diploma. Many departments have established a minimum GED score.

Documents

It is your responsibility to provide proof of education in the form of an official transcript. Submission of a photocopy of a high school diploma, GED Certificate, associates of arts, or bachelor of arts diploma risks rejection on review by the personnel analyst. Submit a complete set of transcripts along with your diploma and/or certificate. Whatever document you forward, submit an official certified copy that has a "raised seal." There will be no uncertainty of its validity.

INCENTIVE PAY

You have heard all of your life from your parents, teachers, coaches, etc., that education is the key to success. Law enforcement is indicative of the value of this advice, because it awards those personnel who have attained higher levels of education. Many departments offer increased pay for these accomplishments. These increments of increase vary in range.

Associates Degree .... 2 percent to 7 percent

Bachelor's Degree .... 5 percent to 12 percent

Master's Degree .... 10 percent to 17 percent

Ph.D. or Law Degree .... up to 22 percent

Remember: Departments will not generally recognize educational achievements unless official transcripts are provided.

As a general rule, if you intend to submit educational credits from military experience, nonaccredited colleges or universities, and foreign colleges or universities, you should have your credentials evaluated by a credential service. It is the responsibility of the candidate to have the units evaluated and turned in with the application. For a credential service, contact the records and admissions office of any university or college in your area and they can provide you with a referral. If you have any questions in regards to your educational level, contact the personnel of the hiring agency and submit your concerns in writing. A written response should be obtained.

Continue to take college level courses until you achieve the degree you seek. Your personal and professional growth will parallel the effort you put forth toward higher education. Imagine yourself on a hiring board and ask yourself, "Which candidate, with equal qualifications, would I hire: the one taking college courses or the one who is not?"

Residency

You will find that most jurisdictions have adopted some form of residence requirement. A residency standard may apply at the recruitment phase or upon appointment. The reasons for residency requirements are varied and some are listed below:

- *Public Relations.* Police administrators committed to community involvement will insist that their police personnel work and reside in the jurisdiction they serve. Similar to the concept of community-oriented policing, officers will get to know and interact with the citizens they serve on a one-on-one basis, breaking down the barrier of mistrust that may exist between the public and police.

- *Budget.* Monetary reasons add to the justification for residency requirements. Budgets are largely based on the taxes raised. Officers have families, buy groceries, cars, clothing and pay property taxes. These taxes go directly into the budget offsetting the expenditures of providing police services.

- *Response Time.* Police officers are peace officers 24 hours a day. Emergency situations may develop at any time, requiring additional personnel immediately. Police executives must be assured that sufficient forces can be marshalled to effectively deal with any crisis in a minimal amount of time. Therefore, callback responses are directly linked to the distance its personnel reside from the station. To minimize response time, officers may be restricted on where they wish to live.

- *Unemployment Index.* Some departments will include a rigid qualification that only residents of that jurisdiction may apply. Oftentimes, city, county, and state governing bodies want only their own citizens to have the opportunity to apply, test and be appointed for vacancies within their department. While this clearly shows a commitment to provide employment and advancement opportunities to its citizens, it also serves to greatly slash the available pool of qualified applicants.

As you direct your attention to an agency, ensure that you meet the residency requirement. If you live out of the area, and they only accept applications from residents, direct your energy elsewhere. Most departments will require residency within a given time frame after appointment. A time frame can range from the date of appointment to 12 months. Plan ahead. Are you willing to reside in the jurisdiction that employs you?

Veteran's or Disabled Veteran's Credit Points

An applicant with prior military experience may qualify for veteran's points. The points awarded to an applicant may be five to ten percentage points. Most often, the applicant must have served at least 100 days of continuous active military service and received an honorable discharge from service. Typically, military reserves or national guard service without at least 180 days of continuous active duty service will not be eligible for veteran's points. To determine whether you qualify, the guidelines representative of most agencies are included. Also, you must have served on full-time active duty, other than active duty for training, in the Armed Forces of the United States during:

World War II .... 12/7/44 to 12/31/46

Korean conflict .... 6/27/50 to 1/31/55

Vietnam conflict .... 1/1/63 to 5/7/75

Persian Gulf conflict .... 8/2/90 to Date Hostilities End

Or if you have received:

The Honorable Forces Expeditionary Medal
Naval Expeditionary Medal
Marine Corps Expeditionary Medal

For:
Hostilities in Lebanon .... 6/1/83 to 12/1/87

Hostilities in Grenada .... 10/23/83 to 11/21/83

Hostilities in Panama .... 12/20/89 to 1/31/90

To receive disabled veteran's credit, in addition to the above, you must be in receipt of, or be entitled to receive, 10 percent (at least) compensation from the Veterans Administration for a disability incurred during the time of war or during the above-listed conflicts. The Veterans Administration must also certify that the disability is permanent. If it is not permanent, you must have been examined by the Veterans Administration within one year of the establishment of the hiring list for the agency to which you are applying

As you prepare your search for employment in the criminal justice field, your military background is an important personal indicator of character, traits, and loyalty. Use this to your advantage. Be ready to submit the required documents to take advantage of the veteran's points available. Documents that may be requested include:

- DD214—long form

- Military discharge papers

Be sure that the photocopies are legible and accurately reflect the pertinent dates and type of discharge (as noted above).

Equal Employment Opportunities

Under the protection of the United States Constitution, inclusive of the Bill of Rights, prevailing case law, and federal and individual state statutes, you are guaranteed the right to fair opportunities in search of employment. All law enforcement agencies must comply with the above mentioned parameters.

You must be considered for employment without regard to race, religion, color, national origin, sex, political affiliation, or age. Due to the nature of law enforcement, some exceptions are available to hiring agencies.

Disability

If you have a disability which may interfere with your ability to take an entrance examination without special accommodations, amanuensis, or other assistance, you should submit a written request for specific special accommodations to the hiring agency's personnel office. Many times, a request such as this requires a 30-work day notice. Also, you may be required to have a physician or agency authorized for that purpose corroborate the specific nature of your disability and justify the need for the special accommodation you are requesting.

CHAPTER FOUR

MEDICAL AND PHYSICAL QUALIFICATIONS

A successful career as a law enforcement officer demands that its members to be physically suited for the rigors of the job. Officers must be prepared to perform all of the strenuous duties they may face in any given tour of duty. The unexpected strength and endurance required to physically subdue a violent suspect, pursue a fleeing felon, and withstand exposure to extreme weather conditions for extended periods of time necessitate that candidates pass certain minimum physical requirements.

Hiring agencies have a responsibility to the citizens they serve to ensure that the police officers they place on the streets are not only capable of performing all police functions, but also do not represent a physical liability to the department. A physically unfit officer may risk the safety of a victim who is depending on the responding officer. The unsuitable officer is more prone to injury and illness, hastening the loss of the officer to sick leave, worker's compensation claims, or early medical retirement. And, ultimately, an officer's life may be lost if he/she is incapable of fulfilling the physical demands required.

Consequently, you should anticipate meeting certain physical qualifications. Every department's requirements vary to some degree. However, there are basic minimums that must be met. Civil liability to the hiring authority is so great in this area that it's reasonable to accept the premise that if you fail to meet a definite prerequisite, there is little reason to even apply.

Prudent advice is to examine the requirements of your agency of choice well before you begin the testing process. Recruitment officials will provide those minimum requirements upon request. If you have a particular concern, submit your concern in writing and await the response. Oftentimes, the recruitment unit may not have the specifics you are seeking and will refer you to their personnel department, human services or office of risk management.

Sadly, some applicants are fearful and hesitant to inquire into a physical limitation they may have, believing they will be rejected before they are ever given the opportunity to compete in the testing process. First of all, the initial acceptance of the application rarely involves a review of the applicant's physical qualifications. You have nothing to fear by asking for information. Further, if you do have a medical disorder, and fail to meet the minimum requirements, you will most certainly be dismissed in the selection process anyway. With a little effort at the front end, you will assure yourself that you meet the physical requirements before the testing process begins. Why risk the time, effort and expense of testing if you sincerely doubt your ability to satisfy the physical requirements?

Common characteristics of police applicants are that they are young and healthy. Quite frankly, few applicants truly know precisely how healthy they really are. Even though an applicant does not exhibit symptoms of illness or impairment, it does not mean that an undisclosed condition will not surface during the physical examination required by the hiring agency. A wise applicant will recognize this issue in advance and take steps to insure he/she is indeed healthy. It is recommended that you consult your family physician, explain your aspirations and undertake a complete physical examination. Your physical exam should also include testing of your vision, hearing, and complete blood analysis. Once you are in receipt of a "clean bill of health," you can proceed, knowing there is little chance of disappointment later in the testing process.

As previously noted, standards will vary from agency to agency. Should a condition preclude you from applying at one department, it doesn't necessarily mean that you won't qualify for another. Offered below is a variety of standards collected from a random sampling of various law enforcement agencies. Any one, or combination of, minimum standards may apply:

General Vision
- 20/40 in the strong eye and 20/70 in the weak eye, correctable with eyeglasses or contact lenses to be 20/20 in both eyes; or 20/70 in the strong eye and 20/100 in the weak eye, correctable to 20/20 in both eyes with soft contact lenses.

- Soft contact lenses users are not subject to uncorrected vision standards if they have experienced successful long-term (6 months) daily use of soft contact lenses which corrects vision to 20/20 in each eye. Some departments require one year of use of soft contact lenses.

- 20/20 uncorrected vision or 20/20 corrected by glasses or hard contact lenses if uncorrected vision acuity is 20/80 or better; or 20/20 corrected by soft contact lenses if uncorrected acuity is 20/20 or better.

Distance Vision

- Uncorrected, not less than 20/100 in each eye. Applicant must have corrected vision of 20/20 in the strong eye.

Near Vision

- Corrected or uncorrected must be sufficient to read print the size of typewritten characters. The ability to distinguish basic colors as well as shades of color, is required, as is normal peripheral vision.

Color Vision

- Adequate to perform essential job tasks as measured on the Farnsworth D-15 Test.

- Must be free from color blindness and any other abnormalities.

Peripheral Vision

- A minimum visual field of 70 degrees.

RK Surgery

- If you have had RK surgery, and you do not wear contact lenses or glasses, your vision must be 20/40 or better in your worst eye.

- If you have RK surgery, your vision with or without contact lenses must be 20/40 or better. Your surgery must have been performed at least one year prior to the date of the medical exam (documentation will be required).

- Orthokeratology treatment is not acceptable. Candidates must have discontinued treatments for at least 12 months prior to the medical exam. Examinations will then be made on a case-by-case basis.

Hearing

- Using an audiometer for measurement, there should be no loss of 30 or more decibels in each ear at the 500, 1,000, 2,000, and 3,000 Cycles Per Second (CPS) levels.

- Pure tone hearing thresholds in the worst ear that exceed 25 decibels without amplification required may be cause for further evaluation and/or disqualification.

- Corrected hearing must be within 75 percent of the normal range, with not less than 90 percent speech discrimination.

Speech

- Diseases or conditions causing in indistinct speech may be disqualifying.

Extremities and Spine

- Deformities or diseases of the extremities and spine that interfere with the full performance of duties may be disqualifying.

Respiratory System

- Any chronic disease or condition affecting the respiratory system which would impair the full performance of duties may be disqualifying (e.g., conditions which would result in reduced pulmonary functions, shortness of breath, or painful respiration).

Cardiovascular System

- The following conditions lead to disqualification: organic heart disease (compensated or not); hypertension with repeated systolic readings of 150 or over and diastolic readings of 90 or over; symptomatic peripheral vascular disease; and severe varicose veins.

Gastrointestinal System

- Diseases or conditions of the gastrointestinal tract that require rigid diets or interfere with full performance of duties may be disqualifying.

Genitourinary Disorders

Chronic symptomatic diseases or conditions of the genitourinary tract which interfere with the full performance of duties may be disqualifying.

Nervous System

Applicants must possess emotional and mental stability with no history of a basic personality disorder. Applicants with a history of epilepsy or convulsive disorders must have been seizure-free for the past two (2) years without medication, and must meet requirements for operating a motor vehicle.

Endocrine System

Insulin-dependent diabetes may be disqualifying.

Hernias

Inguinal and femoral hernias, with or without the use of a truss, may be disqualifying. Other hernias may be disqualifying if they interfere with performance of duties.

Miscellaneous

Though not mentioned specifically, any disease or condition which interferes with the full performance of duties or any disorder which threatens the health and safety of others may be disqualifying.

Height and Weight Requirements

More and more law enforcement agencies are abandoning a traditional height and weight standard for both men and women police applicants. Absent prescribed standards, most departments will merely require that an applicant's height be in proportion to his/her weight. The physical agility testing is a balancing factor to ensure that an applicant is physically capable of performing the duties of a law enforcement officer.

The departments that do maintain a height and weight minimum standard chart will normally not deviate from the standard. Provided is one such example of a sequential height and weight standard, applicable to men and women. Use this as a guide only. Departments will vary greatly!

Male Height and Weight Chart

Feet	Inches	Ttl. Inches	SM Frame −10%	SM Frame	SM Frame +10%	MD Frame −10%	MD Frame	MD Frame +10%	LG Frame −10%	LG Frame	LG Frame +10%
5	2	62	115	128-134	147	118	131-141	155	124	138-150	165
5	3	63	117	130-136	150	120	133-143	157	126	140-153	168
5	4	64	119	132-138	152	121	135-145	160	128	142-156	172
5	5	65	121	134-140	154	123	137-148	163	130	144-160	176
5	6	66	122	136-142	156	125	139-151	166	131	146-164	180
5	7	67	124	138-145	160	128	142-154	169	134	149-168	185
5	8	68	126	140-148	163	130	145-157	173	137	152-172	189
5	9	69	128	142-151	166	133	148-160	176	139	155-176	194
5	10	70	130	144-154	169	136	151-163	179	142	158-180	198
5	11	71	131	146-157	173	139	154-166	183	145	161-184	202
6	0	72	134	149-160	176	142	157-170	187	148	164-186	207
6	1	73	137	152-164	180	144	160-174	191	151	168-192	212
6	2	74	140	155-168	185	148	164-178	195	155	172-197	217
6	3	75	143	158-172	189	150	167-182	200	158	176-202	222
6	4	76	146	162-176	194	154	171-187	206	163	181-207	227

Female Height and Weight Chart

Feet	Inches	Ttl. Inches	-10%	SM Frame	+10%	-10%	MD Frame	+10%	-10%	LG Frame	+10%
4	10	58	92	102-111	122	98	109-121	133	106	118-131	144
4	11	59	93	103-113	124	100	111-123	135	108	120-134	147
5	0	60	94	104-115	127	102	113-126	139	110	122-137	151
5	1	61	95	106-118	130	103	115-129	142	112	125-140	154
5	2	62	97	108-121	133	106	118-132	145	115	128-143	157
5	3	63	100	111-124	136	109	121-135	149	118	131-147	162
5	4	64	103	114-127	140	112	124-138	152	121	134-151	166
5	5	65	105	117-130	143	114	127-141	155	123	137-155	171
5	6	66	108	120-133	146	117	130-144	158	126	140-159	175
5	7	67	111	123-136	150	120	133-147	162	129	143-163	179
5	8	68	113	126-139	153	122	136-150	165	131	146-167	184
5	9	69	116	129-142	156	125	139-153	168	134	149-170	187
5	10	70	119	132-145	160	128	142-156	172	137	152-173	190
5	11	71	121	135-148	163	130	145-159	175	140	155-176	194
6	0	72	124	138-151	166	133	148-162	178	142	158-179	197

CHAPTER FIVE

DRUG TESTING

Pre-employment drug screening is now pervasive throughout most of the U.S. work force. Drug screening was originally intended to ensure that airline pilots, train engineers, public transportation drivers, and other workers in areas where public safety is a concern were not under the influence in the performance of their duties.

The question of one's right to privacy never fails to surface when the subject of pre-employment drug testing arises. Under federal law, employers are generally afforded considerable latitude to consider criminal history and past criminal conduct to determine an applicant's fitness for law enforcement employment. In *New York Transit Authority vs. Blazer*, the U.S. Supreme Court upheld a general policy against employing persons who use drugs in "safety sensitive" jobs. The ruling affirmed that drug testing is legal if it is job related to the legitimate employment goals of safety and efficiency for "safety sensitive" positions.

The need to address illegal drug use in law enforcement is obvious. There are three sets of circumstances of drug use that are of interest to police officials:

- Pre-employment drug screening

- Past drug use and the background investigation

- Illegal drug use on the job

Only the first two will be addressed. As to the third, it is surely a public concern. According to some sources, there is belief that current full-time police officers' use of controlled substances is as high as 10 to 20 percent. If this is true, it is staggering. It wasn't long ago that a large south Florida law enforcement agency was stunned by a drug scandal. The chief of police of that agency admitted that one-tenth of his sworn personnel were "unfit" cops.

For purposes of the hiring process, issues of substance abuse can be divided into two general categories:

1) Use of illegal controlled substances; and/or

2) Excessive or improper use of substances (alcohol, prescription medications, etc.)

If use is identified as problematic, it could be a job-related liability. During the background investigation, the investigator will identify if a specific pattern has emerged:

- What was the frequency of use?

- What was the age of the applicant at the time of use?

- Length of abstinence and any extenuating circumstances that may have contributed to use.

Pre-Employment Drug Screening

Most law enforcement agencies ascribe to the principle of drug testing as a condition of employment. The cost of testing is borne by the hiring agency, although there are exceptions wherein the applicant must cover the cost. An applicant will be given a full screen test, meaning detection of opiates (heroin, methadone, morphine, etc.), barbiturates, amphetamines, methamphetamines, marijuana and its derivatives. The test will be conducted by a reputable facility using closely monitored procedures.

There exist a number of pseudo products that lay claim to the ability to neutralize or disguise a potential positive urine test following illegal drug use. If these products interest you in assisting the defeat of a pre-employment drug screening, then a career in law enforcement is not for you.

Past Drug Use and The Background Investigation

It was not long ago that law enforcement held to the strong conviction that *any* illegal drug use would warrant rejection from the recruitment process. Times have changed, however, and recruitment officials have found that upholding this principle was unwise and impractical. Is it in the best interests of the community to arbitrarily deny a highly qualified, motivated, and intelligent applicant because he/she made a single mistake in college? Of course not. Further, law enforcement was forced to reevaluate its stringent standards because over the last fifteen to twenty years, as society has evolved, the pool of available applicants who have not used controlled substances has become seriously limited.

Every law enforcement agency establishes its own standard of acceptance regarding past illegal drug use. It is not possible to provide an accurate standard which may constitute an automatic disqualification from the selection process. However, random samples of typical minimum standards commonly used by law enforcement agencies in hiring is provided. You may be disqualified for:

- Any use whatsoever of heroin

- Any use whatsoever of hallucinogens (LSD, PCP, etc.)

- If you have ever engaged in the cultivation, manufacture, sale or trafficking of illegal drugs

- Any use of illegal drugs in the last two years

- Any more than occasional past use of marijuana

- Any more than isolated past experience with cocaine, methamphetamines, barbiturates or prescription drugs

- Any use whatsoever of "crack" cocaine

- Any use of illegal drugs within 12 months preceding the date of application

- Any use of illegal drugs within the last two years except— eligibility if no use within the last 12 months and provide proof of successful completion of a medically approved rehabilitative program

- Frequent use of marijuana (ten times within two years of date of application)

- Within three years preceding the date of application, having illegally used controlled substances or dangerous drugs other than marijuana

If these issues are a concern to you, it would be prudent to contact the hiring agency to obtain their restrictions in advance. For the most part, past drug use standards are rigidly enforced. Few, if any, exceptions are granted.

Chapter Six

WRITTEN EXAMINATION

The written examination is a component of the overall selection process. A wide diversity of subjects are found in tests throughout the country. The principal purpose is to eliminate the candidate who fails to possess the necessary skills to perform the duties of a law enforcement officer. Therefore, testing criteria will seek out the candidates who possess problem-solving and decision making skills and who are capable of data and rule interpretation. Also necessary is the ability to understand instructions, accurately observe, exercise sound judgment and employ simple common sense. Applicants will be tested on mathematical proficiency, memory retention, listening and learning skills and reading comprehension. The applicant must demonstrate efficiency in vocabulary, grammar and writing skills which are necessities in every phase of law enforcement.

Day of the Test

The written test will generally be the first phase of the selection process. You have invested countless hours of study and preparation, and now it is time to show what you know.

You are strongly urged to know *exactly* where to report and how to get there. Plan accordingly. Have backup travel arrangements in the event you encounter car trouble. Obtain the bus routes and time schedules in case you must travel by public transportation.

Preparation begins the night before. You need to be physically rested and mentally alert. Make sure you get a good night's rest. On the day of the test, eat a nourishing breakfast and minimize caffeine and nicotine intake. Both are stimulants, and the last thing you need is something to elevate your central nervous system. Remember, nervousness is expected.

Arrive early enough to relax and gain your composure. Have in your possession the following items:

- Photo identification
- Notice to report for examination
- Ballpoint pen
- Two #2 pencils with erasers
- Examination fee (if required)
- Wrist watch

As the test is explained by the examination proctor, listen carefully to all of the instructions. If portions of the test are timed, place your wrist watch in front of you so you can easily monitor the time remaining. As you open the test booklet, read the directions carefully and comply fully.

Basic Test-Taking Rules

1) Neatly print your name on the answer sheet.

2) Blacken the boxes completely.

3) Mark only one answer per question. If an Autoscan is used, it is only going to accept one answer. If two or more are marked, it will be scored as incorrect.

4) If you change an answer, erase it *completely*.

5) If your test is being timed, use your time wisely.

6) Insure you have not skipped a question inadvertently. If you do, chances are that every answer will then be out of sequence.

7) Upon initial review of the questions, answer those you know. Difficult questions should be skipped. Do not waste valuable minutes struggling with the hard questions. You can return to those questions once the remainder of the test is completed.

8) Practice the principle of the process of elimination. If you can eliminate two answers that you know are wrong, you are left with only two choices. Your odds are now 50/50 that you will guess the right one.

9) Use all of the time you are allowed. There are no points for being the first to finish, and you surely will not impress anyone by being the first to leave.

10) Once finished, conduct a systematic review of your answers. As already noted, check to be sure your answers are in proper sequential order. Have you answered *all* questions? Have you completely filled in all of the answer boxes?

Types of Test Components

Reading Comprehension Questions
Law enforcement is governed by local, state and federal statutes. Departmental procedures, priorities, mission statements and discipline are established by policies and procedures which are rigidly enforced. Law enforcement officers must possess the intellect to read, and comprehend pertinent written materials. Assessing an applicants ability, in this regard, begins with the written test. Written tests are validated by personnel analysts for applicability for the position being tested. As a general rule of thumb, reading comprehension and vocabulary examinations are based on a tenth grade reading ability.

You may be given a prepared narrative, normally describing a police investigation. The report will be detailed with facts, events, time frames, locations, and activities of suspects, victims, witnesses and investigating officers. The story will be extensive, but not so complicated that it cannot be understood.

After a set time limit has expired, the story will be retrieved. The applicant will not be allowed to take notes. The test will then commence with a series of questions relating to various elements of the story.

Helpful hint: As you read the story, visualize the events as they unfold. Assign name recognition to the various characters in the story. Study the principle of who, what, when, where, why, and how as you begin to assemble the facts in your mind. Do not attempt to memorize the entire story. Identify the essence of the story, important facts, and the significant actions of the characters. If time allows, before your story is collected, ask yourself what it is you have read and restate it to yourself silently.

As you answer each question, process it thoroughly. Do not read more into it than is there. Identify the question and what it is asking. If you are able to recollect the chronological order of events in the story, one or two of the possible answers may be eliminated. They may be out of time sequence. If you begin to confuse events as you recall the story, anxiety is beginning to take a toll. Stop! Take a deep breath, momentarily distract your thinking to a pleasant and peaceful memory. Now, rethink the events in your mind. Go back to the question where you began to have trouble. Your recollection of the story may surprise you. *Caution—If the test is being timed, you must use time management wisely!*

Multiple Choice Questions

The dominant contents of pre-police service written tests consist of multiple choice questions. Just as it is true with other segments of the testing phase, practice can facilitate an improved score for the applicant who prepares.

At the end of this chapter, two books are recommended as suggested reading. Both contain hundreds of practice multiple choice questions typical of those found in many written police tests. Successful test taking is often determined by repetition. The more opportunities you have to take written tests, the better you will do. In addition to practice, the following helpful hints can be productive:

√ **Read the directions.** Do not assume that you know what the directions are. Make sure you read and understand them. Note if there are different directions from one section to another. The days of "trick" questions are gone. Do not read between the lines. Choose your answer based on your base of knowledge.

√ **Be careful marking your answers.** Be sure to mark your answers in accordance with the directions on the answer sheet. Be extremely careful that:

• You mark only one answer for each question.

• You do not make extraneous markings on the answer sheet.

• You completely darken the allotted space.

• You completely erase any answer that you wish to change.

√ **Read each question carefully.** Know exactly what is being asked.

√ **Read all the choices before choosing an answer.** Don't make the mistake of falling into the trap that the best distractor, or wrong answer, comes before the correct answer. Read all the choices.

√ **Skip questions that are difficult.** Complete the easier questions and come back to the ones that give you trouble.

√ **Never leave any questions unanswered (blank), unless the instructions indicate that a penalty for wrong answers.** In almost all police officer examinations, you do not lose credit for wrong answers. In this case, guess at any questions you are not sure of. However, in rare instances a penalty is assessed for wrong answers. Because this would be explained in the instructions, be sure to read them carefully.

√ **Watch for *unconditional trap words.*** Be alert for words that may be too restrictive to apply. Examples of *unconditional* words: never, always, only, none, will, must, or shall. These words will often indicate a narrow, unconditional option as an answer. These will likely be inserted to *mislead* the test taker.

√ **Look for *conditional words* that may indicate a viable option within the answer.** Examples of *conditional* words: usually, sometimes, maybe, commonly, frequently, most often, may, can, and might. These words tend to offer a solution rather than an automatic response.

√ **Eliminate the known wrong answer.** If you can eliminate one wrong answer, your range of possible answers is reduced.

√ **Do not believe in myths.** Examples: There are more B and C answers than A and D answers. There are an equal amount of A, B, C, D answers, but randomly arranged. Your answers are to be based on your knowledge or best assessment and not random column answers.

√ **Use time management wisely.** When the test begins, do a quick mathematical equation:

Step 1: Count the number of questions on the test.

Step 2: Divide this number by the minutes allowed.

Step 3: This will give you the approximate amount of minutes to spend on each question.

Step 4: Use this as a guide. Pace yourself.

√ **Best guess rule.** If you simply have no clue to the answer, consider:

- Process of elimination of all known wrong answers.

- Scrutinize answers with *unconditional* words.

- Carefully consider answers with *conditional* words.

- If still unsure, go with your first instinct.

Observation/Memory Recall Testing
According to the New Lexicon Webster's Dictionary, *memory* is defined:

". . .the faculty in which sense impressions and information are retained consciously or unconsciously in the mind and subsequently recalled; a person's capacity to remember."

Q. Is the ability to recall minute details important to the officer on the beat?

A. Absolutely. Every shift of every work day, patrol officers are inundated with BOLO's (Be On The Look Out's), teletypes, crime broadcasts, mug shots, composite drawings of wanted suspects and intelligence reports. The ability to recall details involving criminal activities is vital.

It is for this reason that many law enforcement agencies have incorporated memory recall examinations in their testing process. The capacity for memory recall varies greatly from individual to individual. Some people must rely on total memorization in order to recall details. Some will rely on the use of acronyms to refresh their memory, while others may relate information to personal experiences or references to retain important details. Others just do the best they can.

Q. Can you improve your memory?

A. It is not known. Some entrepreneurs believe so and offer expensive mail order home study programs. An alternative is to practice basic principles of memory pictorial recall.

A common instrument in the testing process is the use of a photograph. The picture may be of a crime scene, a common street corner with significant pedestrian and vehicle traffic, or a series of mug shots.

Q. Is the test designed for the applicant to recall every minute detail?

A. No, but that is the problem. You must figure out which details are important and which you will be tested on.

Sample Exercise: The person giving the test will pass out a photograph. Applicants will not be allowed to take notes. You will be allowed to view the picture for a limited amount of time (two to five minutes). The picture will be retrieved after the allowed time has expired. You will then open your test booklet and answer a series of questions pertaining to the content of the photograph.

One way to improve your recall is to separate the scene into two (2) subject matters and then compartmentalize your observations.

1) What was the primary subject matter in the picture?

2) What are the peripheral objects and background activities?

For example: The photograph is a crime scene. The victim is lying in close proximity to a parked car, witnesses are nearby and uniformed officers are protecting the crime scene. The background may consist of street signs, pedestrians, a clock, etc.

Helpful Hints
- Visualize the scene and create mental impressions of the primary subject matter and background details.

- If possible, assign name recognition to characters (i.e., the victim resembles a close friend; the witnesses resemble neighbors, co-workers, or former teachers); the street sign is the name of your home state (i.e., Colorado Avenue).

- Study the principle of who, what, why, where, when, and how and try to answer these as you visualize the photograph.

Strategies for Recall/Memory Recall Testing

√ **Use association to remember.** Don't rely exclusively on rote memory to remember all the items in the picture.

√ **Concentrate until the booklets or photos are collected.** The time between the closing of the memory booklets and the answering of the questions is the most critical time of all. It is imperative that you maintain your concentration during this time. Inexperienced test taker's often forget what they just observed!

√ **Write down everything you recall from the pictorial scene as soon as you can.** After the memory booklet is collected, there will be a delay before you are permitted to open the test booklets and begin taking the examination. Be sure you continue to concentrate ; however once the signal is given to begin the examination, write down, all that you can remember from the pictorial in an outline format. Utilize a sequential format:

- ■ What did I observe? What type of crime was in progress? What are the visible injuries to the victim? What was the proximity of the weapon to the victim, to the suspect? What are the number of witnesses and their locations?

- ■ Observe all readable matter applicable to the pictorial? What was the caliber of the recovered weapon? What was the vehicle make and model? Was the license plate number visible? What were the street signs and number? How many uniformed officers were at the scene?

■ Note the unusual. Is a clock visible? If so, what time did it show? What was the seasonal setting (i.e., victim wearing a winter overcoat, visible snow tires on a nearby vehicle, etc.) Note any open doors, broken windows, or anything that would be out of the ordinary.

Again, practice can improve your memory recollection. The books recommended at the end of this chapter contain memory recall practice tests. As noted throughout this book, preparation is essential to your success.

The Writing Skills Test

While not widely used, this kind of testing is used by the more progressive, well-funded law enforcement agencies. Law enforcement activities are based on record's retention. The ability to write an accurate and understandable crime report is critical to successful performance of the job. Therefore, the logic for this kind of testing is obvious.

Procedure:

Certain variations will occur. However, a typical scenario is provided. The applicant will review a videotape of a police officer receiving and responding to a call reporting a specific crime. He/she will be able to hear and see the officer interview the victim of this crime. The video may last from three to five minutes, and the applicant may be permitted to view the video several times.

Based on what was seen and heard in the video, the applicant will be asked to complete a typical crime report. The report will be evaluated on accuracy, completeness and neatness. It will also be evaluated on the correctness of spelling, punctuation, and grammar, as well as clearness of thought. Clarity to the reader requires that the written product be presented in such a manner that it flows sequentially and can be easily followed. Because of the subjectivity involved in evaluating this kind of test, it is often scored on a pass/fail basis.

Problem Solving Assessment Center

This process, similar in context to the B-PAD psychological test (see Chapter 10) is often used independently in the selection phase.

The purpose is to assess the applicant's decision-making skills, observation skills, listening skills, reading comprehension, writing abilities and problem solving skills. What makes this testing unique is that the applicant's capabilities are assessed while he/she is engaged in strenuous physical activity.

The applicant will first run for 12 minutes, followed by a series of instructions at a series of stations. As the test progresses, the physical demands may include ascending and descending stairs, entering and exiting an automobile and a combination of 25-yard sprints, kneeling, walking, and lifting objects, all while maintaining verbal communication with test proctors.

Mathematical Test Questions

Basic mathematical questions will almost always be included in pre-service police testing. Applicants who have been out of school for an extended period of time may encounter difficulty with arithmetic questions if not prepared. Practicing many forms of mathematical questions is fundamental to success. If you struggle with formulas pertaining to percentages, fractions, decimals, and basic algebra, then it is vital that you refresh these skills.

√ *Fractions/Percentages/Decimals.* You must be familiar with terms such as numerator, denominator, improper fractions, and mixed and whole numbers.

√ *Linear Equations.* In a test capacity, a linear equation is an equation of a line. Solving questions of this nature requires a basic understanding and application of algebra problem-solving procedures.

√ *Arithmetic Reasoning Questions.* This type of test requires the applicant to analyze and solve problems formulated in both verbal and numeric forms. Typically, a set of events is presented in paragraph form, inclusive of numerical figures. The content must be analyzed in order to set up the problem and mathematically solve it.

Spatial Perception Questions

These test questions tend to be very difficult for most applicants. A solid pattern of a three dimensional figure is shown. A series of patterns are provided as potential answers. You are to choose the pattern which, if folded out like a cardboard box, will match that of the pattern provided. In order to identify the correct answer, you must mentally fit several pieces together without having edges overlap or spaces between the various pieces. If you can perceptualize the diagram and visualize the folding of various angles, then consider yourself fortunate. The reality is, most applicants will struggle with this exercise. And unfortunately, there are few viable methods for improving this ability. The best advice is to simply practice. As noted earlier, there are valuable books on the market which contain spatial perception practice test questions.

Vocabulary

The extent of an applicant's vocabulary skills will determine how well he/she will score on the initial written test. This test will also serve as an indicator of how well he/she will progress throughout his/her career. The reality of law enforcement is that paperwork comprises a large part of an officer's work day. Reports are generated on almost every aspect of an officer's activities. A well thought-out, well-written, concise police report will earn the respect of fellow officers, supervisors, police administrators, and prosecutors. A poorly written, grammatically incorrect report will draw negative attention and responses from those you least want to hear from (your sergeant). The importance of having a competent understanding of the English language cannot be overstated. An officer who is armed with a strong command of grammar, vocabulary and writing skills will find the door wide open for special assignments and future promotions. If you are lacking in these areas, now is the time to upgrade your abilities.

There are countless avenues to pursue in this regard. If you are not yet attending, immediately enroll in junior college level English courses. A well-read applicant is an informed applicant. Reading novels, nonfiction books, text books and periodicals will serve to improve your basic language skills. As you read, keep a note pad close by and write down unfamiliar words. Later, look these words up in the dictionary.

Spelling

One area that is often tested is the applicant's ability to spell. As you assemble your study plan, the necessity to spell correctly must be addressed. A list of words commonly used on entry level tests has been provided for your practice. There is no guarantee that your test will consist of these words; however, these words are of the nature frequently used in law enforcement activities. They are intended to be used as a starting point.

abduction
manslaughter
coming
report
frequency
accelerate
minor
compensation
resist
habeas corpus
accessory
municipal
compress
revocation
hazard
accommodate
mustache
confiscate
rigor mortis
negligent
consistent
seize
hypodermic
admissible
night
cooperative
severely
immoral
advice
oath
crime
siren
indecent
aggravate
occasion
deceive
spine
injury
ammunition
offense

collision
renewal
fracture
abortion
medication
commissioner
resident
gradually
accessible
misdemeanor
complexion
restrain
habitually
accidentally
muscle
confession
right
hemorrhage
adjacent
robbery
homicide
administration
neighborhood
conviction
sergeant
illicit
admitted
nuisance
counterfeit
signal
incarcerate
affidavit
obstructed
deceased
specimen
inflicted
altercation
occurring
defendant
strength

forfeit
abet
marijuana
commercial
residence
garage
accept
miscellaneous
complainant
restitution
habitual
accident
multiple
concealed
revoke
height
acknowledge
narcotics
consent heroin
adjustment
negligence
contributing
separate
hysterical
admission
noticeable
coroner
sheriff
inadequately
advised
obscene
damage
specify
infected
alcohol
occasionally
declaration
sprain
innocence
amphetamine

defense
stripped
insufficient
antiseptic
ordinance
describe
sufficient
interrogation
apprehend
passenger
device
surface
investigation
artery
penalty
discipline
suspicion
jeopardize
assistance
physical
dislocation
testify
jurisdiction
authorize
poison
disturbance
traffic
kidnapped
boisterous
precinct
duress
unnecessary
lacerated
bruised
probation
embezzlement
vehicle
latent
business
prosecution

insubordinate
anonymous
operator
deposition
subpoena
interrogate
application
paraphernalia
developed
summons
intoxicated
arrest
pedestrian
disappearance
suspended
irrelevant
assault
personnel
disguise
temporary
judgment
attendant
plaintiff
district
thorough
juvenile
beyond
possession
duplicate
unconscious
laboratory
bruise
probable
embezzled
valid
larceny
burglary
prosecute
employee
verified

omitted
delinquent
subject
interpret
apparent
parallel
designated
suicide
intersection
argument
patrol
diesel
surveillance
involuntary
artificial
person
discrepancy
suspicious
judge
attempted
physician
distinguished
testimony
justice
autopsy
pornography
division
transfer
knowledge
boundary
prisoner
embarrassed
vagrant
laceration
bureau
prohibit
emergency
venereal
legitimate
careful

equipment	lewd	prostitute
violation	caliber	excessive
liability	psychologist	visible
captain	extradition	license
quarrel	warrant	certificate
lieutenant	reckless	width
character	evidence	liquor
recognize	witness	chief
familiar	loitering	referred

Suggested Books

The following recommended test preparation books contain curriculum to enhance grammar, vocabulary and written communication skills.

1) Schroeder, Donald J. and Frank A. Lombardo, *How to Prepare for the Police Officer Examination*, Barron's.

2) *Police Officer*, ARCO Publishing, MacMillan General Reference, A Prentice Hall MacMillan Company.

Chapter Seven

PHYSICAL FITNESS/AGILITY TESTING

The police recruitment process will include physical fitness testing. Just as preparation is essential to do well on the written examinations and oral board presentation, preparation is imperative to pass the physical fitness test. It serves no benefit for an applicant to do well on the written test and possess impeccable credentials if he/she is unable to meet the minimum standards of the fitness testing. The time to prepare is now.

The importance of proper physical conditioning is critical. Contemplate the significance of the following quote, "The criminal element allows for no weakness." Your life may be at stake if you cannot meet the physical demands of a life-threatening situation. Remember also that physical fitness training in a police academy setting is intense and exhausting. Every week, the training staff will push you harder and longer as the expectations of the conditioning regimen increase.

Many academies experience a student "washout" rate of 50 percent. A vast percentage of premature termination is due to failure to meet the demands of the physical fitness training. Do not underestimate the importance of physical fitness. Failure to properly prepare for the high level of physical demands may result in:

- Failure to pass the entry level testing

- Failure to meet the demands of academy training

- An addition to the grim statistic of officers killed in the line of duty failing to overpower a violent suspect

Basis of Testing

The diversity of testing across the country is quite unique. Most physical fitness tests are valid norm-referenced tests in which each test taker's score is compared to the scores of other individuals in a reference group, rather than measured against a preestablished score. Norm-referenced testing is sometimes referred to as health-based testing. The rationale of health-based testing is that all job applicants should be physically fit to enable them to perform the job satisfactorily with minimum risk of injury. In terms of law enforcement testing, *physically fit* refers to being able to perform a standard battery of physical tasks at a level comparable with others of the same age and sex.

Physical Fitness Definition

The ability to carry out daily tasks with vigor and alertness, without undue fatigue, and with ample energy to engage in leisure time pursuits and to tolerate the above average stresses encountered in emergency situations.

Five specific elements are included to make a well-balanced and comprehensive norm-referenced testing program. These five elements are:

- Cardiorespiratory endurance or aerobic capacity, measured by a 1 1/2 mile run

- Abdominal and lower back strengths, measured by sit-ups

- Muscular strength and endurance, measured by push-ups

- Flexibility, measured by a controlled sit and reach test

- Body composition, or percentage of body fat

Most of the norms for this battery of testing were developed by the Institute for Aerobic Research of Dallas, Texas and provide specific standards based on age and gender. The minimum standard of the twenty-fifth percentile is recommended by experts in the field.

Description and Purpose of Testing Instruments

Cardiorespiratory Endurance Test (1 1/2 mile run/walk). The run is one of the best measurements of cardiorespiratory endurance.

This test requires a nearly exhaustive effort. Individuals should not run to complete exhaustion when taking this test and should use caution in how hard they push themselves. They should not exceed the training standards.

Procedure: Most agencies require applicants to run/walk 1 1/2 miles as quickly as possible, within a specific time limit. Applicants should try to maintain a constant, steady pace. It is strongly recommended that prior to running, applicants perform stretching and warm-up exercises. If chest pain or any unusual discomfort is experienced, the applicant should stop immediately. When the test is completed the applicant should cool down by continuing to walk for at least five minutes.

Muscular Endurance Tests. The sit-up test reflects the muscular endurance of the abdominal muscle groups. The push-up test measures the muscular endurance of the shoulder girdle (deltoids, pectorals, and triceps). *Muscular endurance* is defined as the ability to contract the muscle repeatedly over a period of time. Low levels of muscular endurance indicate inefficiency in movement and a low capacity to perform required police work. Muscular endurance testing must use a standardized time frame to control the endurance effort. This is a form of strength testing (dynamic strength) that requires rigid adherence to proper form to be accurate.

Sit-up testing: The participant starts by lying on his/her back, knees bent, heels flat on the floor. A partner holds the feet flat. The participant then performs as many correct sit-ups as possible in one minute. In the up position, the individual should touch his/her elbows to his/her knees and return to a fully flat lying position before starting the next sit-up. The total number of repetitions completed will be recorded.

Push-Up Test:

Male: Applicant must push entire body, including legs, off floor until the arms are straight. This is the starting position. The applicant must keep back straight at all times, and from the starting position, lower his body until his chest is approximately four inches from the floor, then rise to the starting position and repeat as many times as possible. There is a one-minute time limit. The applicant may rest in the starting position only.

Female: Applicant must push her entire upper body off the floor until arms are straight. The applicant's knees must stay in contact with the floor. This is the starting position. The applicant will lower herself until her chest is approximately four inches from the floor, then push back up to the starting position. There is a one-minute time limit. The applicant may rest in the starting position only.

Flexibility Tests (sit-and-reach test). Flexibility is an important physical attribute for preventing injury. *Flexibility* is defined as the range of possible movement in a joint or group of joints. It is necessary to determine the functional ability of the joints to move through a full range of motion. The sit-and-reach test serves as an important measure of hip and back flexibility. Primarily, the elasticity of the muscles in the back of the legs and trunk is tested in the sit-and-reach position. The sit-and-reach test must be performed with proper form to measure true range of motion.

Procedure: The participant should warm up slowly by stretching the muscles of the legs and lower back. The participant sits on the floor or mat with legs extended at right angles to a line on a testing box. The soles of the feet are flat against the testing box, eight inches apart. The participant extends the arms in front with one hand resting on top of the other, slowly reaching as far as possible and holds the position momentarily; bouncing is not allowed. A partner will hold the knees to prevent them from bending. The distance on the box is recorded; normally the best of three trials is scored.

Body Fat Composition. The skin fold body fat test uses the Lang Caliper to yield results. Agencies with sufficient resources will require the participant to submerge underwater for measurement of body fat. Both methods determine relative leanness or fatness, specifically body composition. The overall goal is to evaluate the quality of body weight (i.e., lean mass vs. fat). Specific parameters for maximum body fat will be available to the participant prior to testing.

CHARTS

Minimum standards for the norm-referenced tests will vary from one agency to another. Samples of testing standards are provided and are based on random averages. These are to be considered as guidelines only. The applicant is encouraged to contact the hiring agency for specific minimum standards and prepare accordingly.

CARDIORESPIRATORY ENDURANCE TEST
(1 1/2 MILE RUN)

Age	Male	Female
20-29	12:18-13:46	14:55-16:21
30-39	12:51-14:31	15:26-16:52
40-49	13:53-15:24	16:27-17:53
50-59	14:55-16:21	17:24-18:44

ABDOMINAL AND LOWER BACK STRENGTHS
(SIT UPS)

Age	Male	Female
20-29	35 - 40	30 - 35
30-39	32 - 36	22 - 27
40-49	27 - 31	17 - 22
50-59	19 - 26	12 - 19

(Note: Chart is based on minimum sit-ups required in a one minute time limit.)

MUSCULAR STRENGTH AND ENDURANCE TEST
(PUSH-UPS)

Age	Male	Female
20-29	29 - 33	23 - 26
30-39	24 - 27	19 - 21
40-52	18 - 21	13 - 15
53-59	13 - 15	12 - 13

(Note: Chart is based on minimum push-ups required in a one minute time limit.)

FLEXIBILITY TEST (SIT AND REACH)

Age	Male	Female
20-29	15.5-17.5	18.5-20.0
30-39	14.5-16.5	17.5-19.0
40-52	13.5- 5.3	16.5-18.0
53-59	12.0-14.5	15.5-17.9

BODY COMPOSITION (% OF BODY FAT)

Age	Male	Female
20-29	15.9-22.4	22.1-27.7
30-39	19.0-24.2	23.1-29.3
40-52	21.1-26.1	26.4-32.1
53-59	22.7-27.5	30.1-35.6

Miscellaneous Testing Standards

The above-mentioned tests may not be the only ones required during the physical fitness testing process. Many departments will incorporate modifications in the form of additional strength tests, and/or obstacle and agility tests. Examples of these variations are provided.

Bench Press (one repetition maximum). This test is performed to determine absolute strength in the chest and arms. The applicant lies in the bench press position and must push his/her percentage of body weight shown in the chart below (one repetition only). A universal type machine is normally used for this event. The score for this test is the maximum number of pounds lifted in one repetition, divided by body weight, which gives the percentage of body weight lifted. The scores listed are the minimum percentage of body weight that must be pressed.

Age	Male	Female
20-29	99%	59%
30-39	88%	53%
40-49	80%	50%
50-59	71%	44%
60 +	65%	43%

Leg Press (one repetition maximum). This test is performed to test absolute strength in the leg muscles. The applicant is required to sit on a leg press machine and completely push forward with his/her legs until the legs are fully extended. The applicant must press a percentage of his/her body weight according to the chart below.

Age	Male	Female
20-29	183%	137%
30-39	165%	121%
40-52	157%	113%
53-59	146%	99%
60 +	138%	93%

Three Minute Step Test. This test is given to test cardiovascular conditioning. The applicant must step on and off a box for three minutes. Pulse rate will be recorded for one full minute *before and after* the test is performed in completion. The pulse rate generally cannot exceed 147 bpm (beats per minute) for males and 171 bpm for females. There is no fitness age group designated in this test.

Police Obstacle, Agility and Strength Test

Example #1

√ During this test, you will run a total of 220 yards, negotiating the following obstacles during the run:

• Climb over a six-foot wall

• Climb through a standard size window opening, 36 inches off of the ground

- Crawl under a platform two feet off of the ground for a distance of eight feet.

- Climb over a four-foot wall.

√ Immediately upon finishing the 220 yards, the applicant must then perform: *17 push-ups and nine sit-ups.*

√ The obstacle course and the required number of push-ups and sit-ups must be completed in: *no more than 90 seconds.*

√ After completing the above events, the applicant must demonstrate the ability to hold a pistol at arms' length and squeeze the trigger once, in the double action mode. This must be done with each arm.

Example #2

Mannequin Drag. You must lift and drag a 125-pound mannequin a distance of 50 feet in 15.5 seconds.

Flexed Arm Hang. You will assume the chin-up position (palms facing you) on a chinning bar while standing on a support. When you indicate that you are ready, the support will be removed from underneath your feet. You must support your body weight with bent elbows for 30 seconds.

Wall Climb. You must approach a six-foot wall from a distance of no closer than 20 feet and get over the wall successfully in ten seconds.

1/2 Mile Run. You must run 1/2 mile in four minutes or less.

Shotgun. Applicant in standing position places the 12-gauge shotgun at his/her shoulder as if to fire. At that point, the shotgun must be dry-fired and cocked four times in a ten second time limit. The barrel of the shotgun must be placed inside a six-inch hole of a wooden test stand, and must not touch the wood.

Handgun Trigger Squeeze and Direction Control. You must pull the trigger six times within ten seconds, right-handed, double-action, with right index finger only. The barrel of the handgun cannot have a directional variance of more than six inches. You must then repeat the exercise with your left hand.

Example #3

You will be required to successfully run a timed obstacle course 440 yards in length. *The obstacle course is a simulation of a foot pursuit and will include:*

1. Seated in a patrol car, you will receive a description of a suspect. You will be wearing a waist belt of approximately the same weight as an equipped Sam Browne gun belt.

2. You pursue the suspect by running up a 20 degree incline and then down a 30 degree slope.

3. Jump across a four foot ditch.

4. Maneuver through cones.

5. Run underneath a sign.

6. Go over a two-foot wall.

7. Go over a four-foot wall.

8. Go through a tunnel.

9. Go under a barrier.

10. Go over a six-foot wall.

11. Run up a flight of stairs.

12. Go down a ladder, touching each rung.

13. Hang on, look over a six-foot wall, and read numbers.

14. Climb through a window.

15. Go through a door.

16. Maneuver through obstacles.

17. Identify suspect from description given at start.

18. Climb through a window.

19. Successfully perform a take-down simulation.

20. Run around a cone.

21. Successfully perform a take-down simulation.

22. Drag a 5' 9", 165 pound mannequin a distance of 50 feet.

You should consult your family physician before you train. A thorough medical examination is recommended. A disabling injury or major illness may preclude you from testing. For liability reasons, some departments will require applicants to provide a physician's statement before participating in physical fitness testing.

If you have been provided a waiver of liability in advance of the testing date, follow the directions carefully. Occasionally, the applicant is required to have his/her signature notarized. Imagine your disappointment if, after many months of grueling preparation, you are turned away on the date of the test for failing to have your signature notarized.

Report to the testing site with photo identification, such as a driver's license or military identification. Arrive early to the testing site. Warm-up and stretching exercises will enhance your performance and prevent injury. Insure your comfort by wearing running shoes, comfortable socks, jogging shorts and a t-shirt. Applicants should be prepared to spend several hours taking the series of tests.

Finally, some agencies will require a testing fee to be paid prior to participating in the test. Inquire in advance and report with the required fee.

Chapter Eight

ORAL BOARD INTERVIEW

What Are They Looking For In An Oral Board?

The Oral Board (OB) or Qualification Appraisal Board (Q.A.B.) is merely another stage in the overall recruitment process, but it is the most critical for both the agency (to weed out the unqualified) and the applicant (your opportunity to show individual strengths).

The primary focus of the oral board process is to establish the applicant's command presence, integrity, initiative, interests, communication skills, tolerance for stress and judgment/decisiveness. It is their opportunity to assess the applicant's desire for professional growth, commitment to the community, whether he or she is people-oriented and has the potential to be a professional law enforcement officer.

At the same time, it is their responsibility to eliminate the unqualified or undesirable. Police agencies are all to familiar with the consequences in hiring and, unfortunately, retaining officers that display excessive force, racial bias and/or questionable integrity and character. There is a principle which states, "Good policing can be just as infectious as police corruption and brutality." With modern police management and a focus on "community policing," these "misfits" or "bad apples" cannot, should not, and will not be tolerated. As previously mentioned, the oral board is just one more step in the process to ensure that only the most qualified professional law enforcement officer is hired.

Demographics and Research

Often, applicants know little more about the city in which they are testing than what merely shows on a map. This is ill advised. Mentally familiarize yourself about the area in which you wish to work. It is not uncommon for an oral board to pop a question that specifically pertains to the department or city. Unless you familiarize yourself and keep abreast of the political atmosphere of that community, you probably will not be able to answer these questions unless you conduct your own research before entering the interview.

If you are truly serious about becoming an officer in that community, be prepared to show a hiring authority that you care enough to know the particulars of that community. Educate yourself before the test. Sample issues are:

- What is the population of the city?

- What is the racial climate and how is the department trying to meet the needs of the minority population?

- Are there any particular "high profile" issues presently affecting the community?

- What is the size of the police force?

- Is community policing utilized by the department?

- What is the chief's name, and how long has he held his position?

- What type of government system is in place? (mayoral, city manager, city council, etc...)

- Be prepared to explain what the Uniform Crime Report (UCR) is.

- Has the department experienced an increase or decrease in crime statistics as noted in the UCR?

- What is the unemployment rate?

- Can you name three current members of the United States Supreme Court?

If you believe preparation of this nature is a waste of time, you are mistaken. All of these types of questions, as well as others, have been used many times by oral boards. Answers to these questions are available to dedicated applicant wanting to finish number one on the test. Phone calls to the recruitment division, community relations department, or crime prevention unit will answer most of these questions. A visit to the local library can also provide a wealth of information. If you have access to the Internet, you'll find many facts and figures on the community you are researching.

Rehearsal

There is no doubt that your first oral board will induce a great deal of stress. Unless you have extensive public speaking experience, speaking in front of a hiring board will be a very nerve wracking experience. You do not have to go in blind and watch the chips as they fall. There are proactive measures that you can take to reduce your apprehension and improve your performance.

Speak with fellow students, friends, family members and co-workers that may have already tested for other police agencies. Prepare a list of potential questions. Give each question thorough consideration. Practice your own questions and answers until your responses are delivered confidently.

Next, conduct your interview in front of a mirror. Tape record your responses. There is a very specific purpose for using a mirror. You will be able to practice establishing eye contact with board members as well as detecting any fidgeting. You will be probably be surprised to hear how you sound during an interview. Most times, we are our own worst critic. Critique yourself and modify your responses. Once again, test yourself.

Are you ready for the next level of preparation? Conduct a practice live oral board. Ask friends, co-workers, or relatives to assemble a mock oral board. Provide them with a list of questions, and ask them to think of their own spontaneous questions. The purpose of unexpected questions is to confront you with the unanticipated. It will force you to think under pressure, tapping all of you resources and preparedness. This is exactly what you will need to do when it counts most. Inform those helping you of how important this exercise is so as to minimize any joking and jesting. This exercise is as close to the real thing as you will get. It is greatly beneficial to your success.

If at all possible, videotape your performance. Upon review, you may see faults in your performance that can be improved upon. Certain body movements that may distract from your verbal communication may not be noticeable until you see them on tape. You will be looking for:

- Use of voice (command presence)
- Tone of voice
- Rate of speech
- Volume of speech
- Pitch of speed
- Eye contact
- Facial expressions
- Hand gestures
- Breathing rate

The video cameras has forever changed how police departments police themselves(i.e., the Rodney King case). A video camera can be a superb training aid to perfect your oral board performance.

Preparation can pay big dividends. Not only will you begin the process of becoming more at ease speaking in front of a panel, but it will also inspire you to study the pertinent information you may be asked.

Styles of Questions

It is not possible to provide the exact types of questions you will encounter in an oral board, but being familiar with the various kinds of questions will aid you in your preparation. Any one, or combination of, the following maybe encountered:

- *Practical aptitude testing.* Candidates will be tested on their reasoning ability. Questions will be posed for the applicant to analyze hypothetical situations that a police officer might encounter. These questions are based on law enforcement procedures and/or police practices, although hiring boards recognize that applicants lack this base of knowledge. Nevertheless, these questions have merit. They are designed to inquire into how you would handle a predetermined situation. The objective is to place you in a stressful setting, force you to think as quickly as possible, and articulate your answer with "command presence." The oral board will be looking at your ability to handle stress and react instinctively and the intuitive ability to make decisions.

You might be wondering how you are supposed to know how to handle a police situation. You're not. But that does not mean you cannot learn. Maybe you will be asked how to handle a family disturbance or a belligerent drunk driver. So find out! Later in this chapter, suggestions will be made about how to begin the process of learning more about police work. Posing situational questions during an oral board is a very common practice. Prepare. Prepare now.

- *Personal Inventory.* Oral boards using this type of forum are really looking for character traits the applicant has. The board will want to know about your educational level, educational achievements, work history, goals, aspirations, and sincerity for the job. Have you chosen law enforcement as a career or is it merely a job while you are in transition in life? Some typical objective questions may include:

    √   Why do you want to be a law enforcement officer?

    √   What have you done to prepare yourself for this position?

    √   Why have you chosen this police department?

    √   Why should we hire you?

    √   What are your three strongest qualities?

    √   What are your three weakest traits?

    √   What accomplishment in your life are you most proud of?

    √   At your last job, what was your most impressive accomplishment, and your biggest mistake?

You might be asked to comment on your feelings about your present or past employer. It is not that boards want to know about the employer, but rather they want to know how you *feel* about the employer. Do not criticize a present or former employer! Police executives want to hire applicants with positive attitudes. Criticizing others conveys the negative message that you are hard to get along with. Do not live in the past. Potential employers care about your future performance. If they ask, describe your past experience in terms of its usefulness to the future and how it can benefit their police department.

Be prepared to summarize these background issues. Arrange your thoughts and put them in writing. Practice responding to these questions until you can deliver the answers calmly and with confidence.

A police officer is a very visible symbol, and law enforcement agencies are involved in various community activities. If you are, or have been, involved in activities, use them to your advantage. Being involved in youth activities such as Boy Scouts, Pop Warner Football, or Little League will be received very favorably by the hiring agency. Certainly, as you compose your closing statement, this community involvement should be included.

How You Dress May Affect Your Score

The premise that "The first impression, leaves a lasting impression" is very important. How you are dressed for the interview may set the stage for how you are perceived by the oral board members. When you walk into the room, you want the board members to see a motivated, aspiring professional. Some may say, "It shouldn't matter how I look, it's what I can do that counts!" But, like it or not, people judge others by the way they look. Your personal image includes everything from style of dress, jewelry, hairstyle, and cleanliness. A phrase often heard in military and police academy settings is, "Look sharp, be sharp!" It begins at the oral board.

If you want to dress casually for work, you need to find a work environment with a relaxed dress code. Effective policing relies greatly upon professionalism. Take a look at how the board members are dressed. They will be dressed in business attire. You may be the best qualified in terms of skills, education and knowledge, but if you do not fit the police officer image, you may not get the job.

Male applicants should wear a suit and tie and/or matching sport coat and tie. Have your dress shirt pressed and starched. Female applicants should wear a business suit or dress. Loud or provocative apparel is not advised. It is best if your color of dress is conservative (i.e., black, brown, navy blue).

Personal hygiene and grooming are equally important. Remember that law enforcement is a highly visible occupation and most police agencies have adopted strict grooming standards. While it may seem unfair, an applicant with long hair is simply going to be received less favorably than an equally qualified applicant with a "politically correct" appearance.

Before your oral board, contact the hiring agency and find out what the grooming standards are. All police agencies have a section in their policy and procedures manual which addresses grooming standards. There are restrictions to length of hair, applicable to both male and female officers. Also regulated are the styles of sideburns, beards and mustaches. If you are serious about a career in law enforcement, now is the time is to conform to the standards that you will be required to meet. As you make your entry into the room for the oral board phase of the application process, the boards' first and lasting impression should be, "Looks sharp!"

The Night Before

Your successful performance at the oral board begins on the night before. It is imperative that you get a good night's rest before your examination. If your current employer requires you to work a graveyard shift the night before the exam, ask for the night off. You must be well rested and well nourished. Eat a well-balanced breakfast the morning of the test. Minimize your caffeine and nicotine intake before the test. Both substances are stimulants and may affect your mental faculties.

The Interview

In times of recruitment, many large metropolitan police department will conduct a multi-phase testing process involving literally thousands of applicants. As these candidates are reduced throughout the selection process, there may still be hundreds of applicants scheduled to take the oral board on the same date as you. In order to control the vast numbers, systems are utilized to ensure chaos does not occur. When you are notified to appear for the oral board tests, you may be given a *notice of appearance*. This is your written permission slip to attend. Without it, you may not be able to participate in the testing. When you receive your notification, place it in a safe location and be sure it accompanies you on the date of your test.

As you walk in the testing room, do so in a confident and polite manner. If you are escorted into the room by a support staff employee, thank him/her as he/she directs you to where you will be seated. The first five minutes of the interview are critical. First impressions are vital. If you do not make a good impression immediately, chances are that you will not be able to recover, however excellent your qualifications may be.

In addition to a gun and baton, an officer's tools of the trade also include a pen and note pad. The oral board is no exception. You should also have a current resume. Place all of these items on the table in front of you. Most oral boards are comprised of three to five board members. There may be a personnel analyst that chairs the test or a board member serving as the spokesperson. When introductions are made, this person will explain how the interview will be conducted. If the physical surroundings permit, shake each board member's hand as greetings are exchanged. Your handshake should be firm but not crushing. If you give a "wet fish" handshake, instead of a solid one, the impression will be that you are timid and ineffectual. As each member states his/her name, repeat it, and say an appropriate "How do you Do?" Before you sit down, hand your resume to the chairperson and state that you brought it for the board's perusal. Be assured that as your interview proceeds, your resume will be passed among the board members, which is exactly what you want. Remember though, a resume does not get the job, the applicant does.

Sit down and take a deep breath. An oral board is going to invoke a deep sense of anxiety and nervousness. This is natural. Hopefully, your practice has helped to minimize the degree of edginess you will experience. Sit up straight and fold you hands in front of you. Keeping your hands folded will prevent you from fidgeting, a distraction to both you and those judging you.

The test will now commence. Normally, each board member will ask a question which will be rotated among them depending on the number of prearranged questions. As each question is posed, make eye contact with the member asking the question. Do not take your eyes off the interviewer as the question is being asked. Listen carefully! If you are unsure or do not understand, ask that the question be restated. The first question is commonly the most nerve wracking. All of your aspirations, training, practice, and dreams have led to this moment. Unless you have ice in your veins, trepidation will permeate every cell in your body. It is time to step up to the plate!

Helpful hint: If you feel the onset of panic, force yourself to think quickly, but rationally. Tell yourself that you are capable and confident. Calm your mind by filling it with comforting images, and give yourself time to think logically.

As you begin to deliver your response, you cannot ignore the rest of the board members; they are scoring you as well. Make eye contact with all of the board members as you speak. It is recommended that you practice the 50/50 Rule—maintain eye contact with the interviewer asking the question 50 percent of the time, and the remainder 50 percent should be focused on the other board members. In a calm and fluid manner scan all board members until you have answered the question. As the second question is asked, again apply the 50/50 Rule to the board member asking the question. This process should be repeated throughout the interview.

Exhibiting proper maturity, body language, tone of voice, and professional presentation skills is essential. A police officer's ability to survive on the street is often based on his/her ability to communicate with the public. Your answers should be clear, concise and direct.

Do not:

- Exhibit an arrogant, cocky, or "know-it-all" attitude
- Argue with a board member

A pleasant personality is welcomed, but a comedian is not. Leave needless humor at home. Do, however, be courteous and respectful. If a question is asked, and you have no idea what the answer is, tell the interviewer that you do not know the answer. Do not try to fool them by pretending you know more than you do. They will see right through you, and it will reflect in your overall score. Remember, you are unschooled in a very complicated field, so you are not expected to have the answers that a seasoned veteran would. Be yourself.

At the conclusion of your interview, you may be asked if you have any questions or you may be asked to make a closing statement. It is professionally acceptable to ask questions about their hiring intentions, number of openings, and an estimated date that offers of employment may be extended. You have a responsibility to your present employer to provide sufficient notice of resignation. The board understands this. Your closing statement should be well thought out. Keep it short. Summarize your qualifications and personal goals, and emphasize your commitment to not only the profession but also the particular agency interviewing you. Convince them that you are goal-oriented and that you look forward to a long and rewarding career with their agency. Do not leave the impression that you will jump at the first offer you receive. Your sincerity may be in question if this feeling is perceived. Police agencies frown on training and developing a young recruit, only to have that officer move on to another agency. As you are excused, thank the board for the opportunity to meet with them. Again, if the surroundings allow, shake each board member's hand as you express your appreciation. Move the chair back to it original position and close the door as you exit the room.

Post-Interview Planning

After you have left the room, get a drink of water, sit down and relax. Its over! It is time to reflect on areas where you were particularly strong and the areas where you need improvement. You may be testing for other departments. Take the time to improve your performance for the next agency.

Take out your note pad and write down the questions, and objectively evaluate your answers. You will know if you did poorly on a particular question. There is no reason to dwell on what was or was not said correctly. Use this experience to prepare and practice for your next oral board.

- Spend time in your local library. There are many books on police techniques, theory, community relations, criminology, constitutional law, search and seizure, laws of arrest, use of force, etc. As you read and research the field, questions you were asked in the oral board will surface. You will be able to reflect on how you can improve your answers.

- Consult with those in the occupation. If you know an experienced law enforcement officer, review the questions you were asked with him/her. Feedback from one who has done the job for years can be invaluable. Use caution however. This may be one person's opinion, and it is not necessarily the best answer to the question. Parroting another person's opinion is not recommended, instead use his/her insights to build upon your own knowledge base.

- Contact a law enforcement agency and request permission to participate in a Ride-Along-Program. Most departments allow citizens to accompany a patrol officer in the field. This is very valuable experience. It will provide an opportunity to observe first hand how an officer handles various types of radio calls.

- Practice. Return to your home and test yourself once again. This time you have more data with which to prepare. You can restructure your practice methods with actual oral board questions. You have additional input from books, answers from those in the field, and personal experience from your ride-along observations. You will be wiser and more knowledgeable. Now you must refine your demeanor and presentation skills. Also, as you practice sample oral board questions, you will lower your anxiety level for the next oral board and improve your performance.

Chapter Nine

AMERICANS WITH DISABILITIES ACT OF 1990

A career in law enforcement tends to attract people from all walks of life. This also includes persons with disabilities. If you are inflicted with a condition that you suspect might disqualify you from employment, it is imperative that you research the matter and understand the law and your rights.

The following information regarding the Americans with Disabilities Act (ADA) of 1990 is not meant to provide only an overview regarding the provisions of the law but rather a legal interpretation. Your condition in question and the flexibility of the law must be determined on a case-by-case basis. You are encouraged to seek definitive guidance and determine your status before you commence with the testing process. The answers to your questions can be found by a collective inquiry with the United States Office of Equal Employment Opportunity, your State agency charged with enforcement of equal employment opportunity issues, the hiring agency's personnel department, or a private attorney knowledgeable in the ADA of 1990.

History

The ADA was signed into law by President Bush on July 26, 1990. The ADA has five "titles" (i.e., sections) which together prohibit discrimination against qualified persons with a disability in the areas of employment, public services and transportation, public accommodations, and telecommunication services.

Before enacting the ADA of 1990, the Federal Rehabilitation Act (FRA) was established in 1973. The FRA of 1973 was designed to promote and expand employment opportunities for handicapped individuals in both the public and private sectors (29 USC 711). The FRA prohibited employers with federal contracts and subcontracts greater than $2,500 from discriminating against handicapped individuals.

In 1990, the ADA became law. Included in the legislation is Title I. The general intent of the ADA is to extend coverage of the FRA of 1973 to private employers and those with federal government ties.

The agency charged with monitoring and enforcing prescribed provisions of the ADA is the United States Office of Equal Employment Opportunity Commission (EEOC).

PURPOSE

The EEOC regulations prohibit employers from discriminating against a qualified individual with a disability in any aspect of employment, including:

• Application	• Promotion
• Testing	• Medical Exams
• Hiring	• Layoff
• Assignment	• Termination
• Evaluation	• Compensation
• Discipline Action	• Leave Status
• Training	• Benefits

Quota is a very controversial term with regard to recruitment. It is noteworthy that neither ADA nor EEOC regulations require preferences favoring disabled individuals, or any resemblance to an employment quota system. Furthermore, the ADA does not relieve disabled employees and applicants from being required to have the ability to perform essential job functions. It does, however, require employers to take certain affirmative measures to accommodate disabled individuals who, apart from their disabilities, are otherwise qualified for employment.

Employer Impact

ADA is applicable to employers with 15 or more employees (effective July 26, 1994). With regard to employment issues, Title II of ADA places all state and local agencies under the auspices of Section 504 of the FRA, whether or not the agency receives federal assistance.

Who is Protected by the ADA?

The ADA prohibits discrimination against **"all qualified individuals with disabilities,"** as well as individuals having a record of being disabled. Individuals who are discriminated against because of an association or relationship with a disabled individual are also protected.

ADA Definitions

Disability: Physical or mental impairment that substantially limits one or more major life activities.

Physical or Mental Impairment: Any *physiological disorder* or condition, cosmetic disfigurement, or anatomical loss affecting one or more of the following body systems:

- Neurological

- Musculosketetal, special sense organs

- Respiratory, including speech organs, cardiovascular reproductive, digestive, genitourinary, hemic, and lymphatic, skin and endocrine

Any *mental or physiological disorder* such as:

- Mental retardation
- Organic Brain Syndrome
- Emotional or mental illness
- Specific learning disabilities

Major Life Activities
Impairment affecting basic functions that the average person can perform with little or no difficulty, including:

- Walking
- Speaking
- Breathing
- Manual tasks

- Seeing
- Hearing
- Learning
- Working

What Conditions are NOT Protected by the ADA?

1. Temporary, non-chronic impairments (broken bones, sprains, flu, obesity and pregnancy)

2. Physical characteristics, such as eye and hair color, dexterity, height, weight, or muscle tone that are not within "normal" range

3. Personality traits that are unrelated to mental or physiological disorders (poor judgment, quick temper, timidity).

4. Sexual behaviors (homosexuality, bisexuality, transvestitism, pedophilia, exhibitionism, voyeurism)

5. Compulsive disorders (gambling, kleptomania, pyromania)

6. Socioeconomic status (poverty, educational level, criminal history)

7. Advanced age (noteworthy, medical conditions commonly associated with age, such as hearing loss and arthritis, *are* covered by ADA)

8. Polysubstance abuse resulting from disorders from current, illegal use of drugs

Common Questions Regarding ADA

Q: Would a medical disqualification from the peace officer selection process constitute, in and of itself, a substantial limitation in the major life activity of working?

A: Maybe. The answer is not entirely clear. The inability to perform a single job does not constitute a substantial limitation in the major life activity of working; rather, an individual must be significantly restricted in the ability to perform either a "class of jobs" or a "broad range of jobs" in various classes (as compared to the average person having comparable training, skills, and abilities).

To determine whether an individual's ability to work is substantially limited, the EEOC will consider the geographical area to which the individual has reasonable access; the job from which the individual has been disqualified, as well as the number and types of jobs using similar training, knowledge, skills and abilities within that geographical area; and the number and type of other jobs not using similar training, knowledge, skills and abilities from which the individual is also disqualified.

Given this, it would seem prudent to assume that all individuals are protected under the ADA if they have been restricted or disqualified from police work due to a physical or mental impairment, regardless of the condition (not withstanding the types of conditions not protected under the ADA).

Q: Who is a "qualified individual with a disability?"

A: To be considered "qualified," an individual with a disability must satisfy the requisite skill, experience and education requirements of the job in question and be able to perform the essential functions of the job (with or without reasonable accommodation).

Q: Would "stress" be considered a protected condition under the ADA?

A: Stress and depression are conditions that may or may not be considered impairment, depending on whether these conditions result from a documented physiological or mental disorder.

Example: A person suffering from general stress because of job or personal life pressures would not be considered to have an impairment. However, if this person is diagnosed by a licensed psychiatrist or psychologist as having an identifiable stress disorder, he/she would have an impairment that may be a disability.

Q: Is it permissible to disqualify an applicant if he/she is found to have a history of illegal drug use, even if he/she is not currently engaging in such drug use?

A: Generally, yes. All employers have the right to seek reasonable assurances that no illegal use of drugs is occurring or has recently occurred so that continuing use is a real, ongoing problem. In addition, law enforcement agencies can impose a qualification standard that excludes those with a history of illegal drug use if it can be shown that the standard is job-related and consistent with business necessities.

Example: A law enforcement agency could argue that such an illegal history would undermine the credibility of an officer for the prosecution in a criminal case.

It should also be noted that those who are not illegally using drugs, but whom are erroneously perceived as being addicts or current drug users, are also protected by the ADA.

Q: Is alcoholism considered a disability under the ADA?

A: Yes. An individual cannot be discriminated against in employment on the basis of past or current alcoholism.

However, an employer may hold an employee who is an alcoholic to the same qualification standards for employment or job performance and behavior that applies to other employees, even if any unsatisfactory performance or behavior is related to the alcoholism of the individual. Furthermore, an employer can restrict the employment rights of an individual if he or she is a "direct threat" to the health and safety of him/herself or others.

Q: Can an applicant be questioned about, or tested for illegal drug or alcohol use?

A: Prior to a conditional job offer, an employer may ask whether an applicant drinks alcohol or whether he/she is currently using drugs illegally. However, the applicant may not be asked if he/she is a drug addict or alcoholic, nor can any inquiry be made regarding history of drug or alcohol rehabilitation program participation.

Testing for illegal drug use is allowed in any selection process; however, tests to determine either the presence of alcohol or the use of prescription drugs would be considered a medical examination and can, therefore, only be required after a conditional job offer is made.

Q: Is the employee or applicant required to provide any proof of his/her stated disability? Must the employer take the person at their word?

A: If the disability is not obvious (i.e., dyslexia), an employer may require the individual to provide documentation of the need for accommodation. However, at the pre-offer stage, the employer should only request documentation related to the need for, and type of, accommodation necessary, rather than detailed information related to the nature and extent of the disability.

Q: If there are several qualified applicants for a job, does the ADA require that the applicant with a disability be hired?

A: NO. The more qualified applicant may be hired. The ADA is only intended to make it unlawful to discriminate against a qualified individual on the basis of a disability.

Q: Are all selection procedures, criteria and disqualification standards that have the effect of disqualifying individuals with disabilities unlawful under the ADA?

A: No. Tests, standards, and other selection criteria that have a disparate impact on (i.e., screen out) disabled individuals are lawful *if* they can be shown to be job-related.

Q: How does the prohibition against pre-offer medical inquiries impact the police officer selection process?

A: There is no discernible impact to the law enforcement agency resulting from ADA.

Reading/writing ability: No changes would appear to be needed except to insure that the time limit, as well as the content of the test itself, is job related.

Q: What types of questions cannot be asked at the pre-offer stage?

A: Prior to making a conditional job offer, applicants may *not* be asked any questions regarding their disability nor any questions about their worker's compensation history. This means that employers cannot ask applicants about the presence or absence of any medical condition, the need for prescription drugs or any other regimen to control their condition(s), nor any questions regarding the nature, severity, duration, etc., of a disability.

Drug Testing

The use of illegal drugs is not protected by the ADA, therefore drug testing can be performed at any point in the selection process. However, inquiries about the applicant's history of illegal drug (or alcohol) use are prohibited prior to a conditional job offer.

Psychological Screening

The ADA's impact on when a psychological screening can be performed is unclear. The EEOC regulations indicate that if the purpose of the screening is to assess mental "traits" (i.e., quick temper, etc.), the assessment can be performed at any point in the process, because traits are not considered disabilities, and are not, therefore, covered under the ADA. However, if the psychological screening in question assesses mental disabilities (i.e., psychosis, depression), then it should be administered post-offer, because individuals with these conditions are protected under the ADA.

Physical Agility Test

The EEOC has determined that physical agility tests are not medical exams, and thus may be given at any point in the selection process. However, the tests must be given to *all* applicants, regardless of disability. In addition, if the tests screen out individuals with disabilities, it must be demonstrated that they are job-related and consistent with business necessity and that satisfactory performance of the tests cannot be achieved with reasonable accommodation.

If an applicant or student (employed or non-affiliated) is given a physical agility test at the pre-offer stage, only very limited medical screening is allowed in order to assure that the test will not harm the applicant. The employer can request that applicants (and/or their physician's) respond to a very restricted inquiry which describes the physical demand of the test, and can ask, "Can this person safely perform this test?" It is also permissible to ask if an individual requires a reasonable accommodation in order to safely perform the test.

ADA Questions

Questions regarding the American Disabilities Act of 1990 may be addressed to:

The EEOC Washington D.C. Office
(800) 669-EEOC
(800) 232-4999

Department of Justice
Office of the Americans with Disabilities Act
Civil Rights Division
P.O. Box 66118
Washington D.C. 20507

References and Resources

(ADA Law, Regulations, and Technical Assistance)

The Americans with Disabilities Act; 42 U.S.C. Section 12101

Equal Employment Opportunity Commission, *Equal Employment Opportunity for Individuals with Disabilities;* Final Rule, 29 CFR Part 1630; Federal register, Vol. 56, No. 144, July 26, 1991, pp. 35726-35756.

Department of Justice, *Nondiscrimination on the basis of Disability in State and Local Government Services*; Final Rule, 28 CFR 35; Federal Register, Vol. 56, No. 144, July 26, 1991, pp. 35694-35723.

Equal Employment Opportunity Commission, *A Technical Assistance Manual on the Employment Provisions (Title I) of the Americans with Disabilities Act*, 1992.

For copies of regulations, technical assistance manuals, etc:

U.S. Equal Employment Opportunity Commission
Office of Communications and Legislative Affairs
1801 L. Street, N.W.
Washington, D.C. 20507
(202) 663-4900

ADA REFERENCES

(PERTINENT TO LAW ENFORCEMENT AGENCIES)

Arnold, D.W. and Thiemann, A.J., "To Test or Not To Test: The Status of Psychological Testing Under the ADA," *Criminal Justice Digest*, Vol. 11, No. 2, February, 1992.

Bosarge, B.B., "Implementing ADA Expected to Cost Law Enforcement Millions in Litigation Fees," *Criminal Justice Digest*, December 23, 1991, Vol. 25, No. 51, pp. 1-9.

Farenholtz, D.W., "The Impact of the ADA on Developing Physical Abilities Standards," *Law and Order*, March, 1992, Vol. 40, No. 3. pp. 63-67.

Chapter Ten

PSYCHOLOGICAL TESTING

If this is your first experience with psychological testing, being informed about what to expect will make the process easier. Just as the importance of preparation was explained in the oral board testing process, the same principle applies to this testing. Being well rested, nourished and relaxed is essential. Above and beyond any other advice, you must conduct every phase with total honesty. Any attempt to mislead, mitigate or falsify either your written or verbal responses will be discovered, and rejection is then inevitable. Research data indicates that psychological testing disqualifies 40 to 60 percent of applicants. Psychological testing is a very controlled procedure. The interviewer will follow specific guidelines. It is not a process that can be hurried. Therefore, plan on spending three to four hours to take the series of written tests and to be interviewed.

The qualified professional administering the tests must have a thorough knowledge of the peace officer's job and how specific mental and emotional factors impact job performance.

Various personality traits are sought. Specific traits considered important in police work include:

- Logical reasoning

- Decisiveness

- Compatibility

- Self-confidence

- Sensitivity

- Diplomacy

- Stress tolerance

- Organization

- Positive motivation

- Behavioral flexibility

- Command presence

Psychological testing attempts to identify not only a healthy personality, but also a personality which will remain healthy. Psychological suitability will be determined on the basis of objective psychological test score information interpreted by the qualified professional. Most testing forums use a *minimum* of two psychological tests. One test instrument may be conducted in such a manner as to identify patterns of abnormal behavior. The second test may be oriented towards assessing relevant dimensions of normal behavior.

Clinical Interview

In combination with the use of validated testing instruments, a clinical interview may be incorporated in the total assessment process. The value of a clinical interview cannot be overstated. Yet, it is not always mandated. A clinical interview is a time consuming in-depth process and a very expensive tool. Many locals hiring agencies cannot afford the cost of a professional's hourly rate to conduct the clinical interview.

If feasible, the clinical interview provides the professional with the opportunity to integrate test data and life history information into an overall framework. In conjunction with the total process, the traits uncovered may include:

- Ability or inability to handle stress
- Interpersonal skills
- Emotional control
- Violent or aggressive behavior

It is important to identify a violent or aggressive personality. All too frequently in the media we witness the unfortunate consequences of not being able to do so. Although clinical interviews alone lack the validation to support selection decisions, combined with test data, they can provide a more complete picture of the applicant.

When validation tests result in inconclusive determination, or a recommendation is made to disqualify an applicant, most agencies require that a clinical interview be conducted. The clinical interview will serve to verify and/or clarify test dimensions.

TEST MEASUREMENT Tools

Testing components used across the country will vary greatly. While listing all of the test instruments is not possible, a sampling of the common instruments used, along with general explanations, are provided. These are not offered as clinical definitions, but rather as informational guidelines only.

Behavioral Personal Assessment Device (B-PAD)

The B-PAD is a frequently used tool and, in some instances, is used in place of the oral board process. The B-PAD exercise is proving to be one of the more progressive instruments in the police recruiting process. Its uses are many. The applicant's performance may reveal problem solving ability, judgment under pressure, decisiveness, diplomacy and their degree of "genuine interest" in people.

The B-PAD is a video test in which a candidate views up to 8 video screens that require the candidate to respond as if he was the officer at the scene. For those who are inexperienced at police work and concerned, be assured that the B-PAD is *not* a test of police procedure. Rather, it is a reflection of the candidate's interpersonal confidence in dealing with different types of people in various situations typically encountered by police officers. The B-PAD process assesses an applicant's ability to effectively evaluate the situation, develop a plan of action, follow-through and bring the situation to closure.

Minnesota Multiphasic Personality Inventory-2 (MMPI-2)

The MMPI-2, is a 608 item test. Like its original predecessor, the MMPI-2 was designed for use with adults and is used extensively in police psychological testing.

The applicability of the test covers a vast range of personality trait predictors. Depression, obsessive-compulsive tendencies, suicide potential, anger and low self-esteem are some. The MMPI-2 also contains unique testing skills that measure alcohol and drug problems, the likelihood of these problems to arise in the future, and a theoretical-based criteria for testing psychological maturity.

Sixteen Personality Factor Questionnaire Fifth Edition (16pf)

This testing tool, often used for psychological testing of pre-service police recruits, is designed to predict a broad range of personality traits and a wide range of behaviors. It is particularly effective in predicting social skills which are necessary for public service.

The test takes 25 to 50 minutes and consists of 185 questions with a multiple choice format. There are 15 test questions at the end of the test that measure reasoning ability. Test applicators encourage subjects to answer all questions and to choose the first response that comes to mind rather than spending too much time an any one particular question.

Thematic Apperception Test (T.A.T)

The TAT is similar in context to the Rorschach Test (inkblot), but unlike the Rorschach Test, with which it is often administered, there is no quantitative scoring technique. The TAT is a projective instrument used as a diagnostic tool. Its sole purpose is to induce the thoughts, attitudes, and feelings of the subject as he/she narrates stories based upon pictures.

The test consists of 10 picture cards for women, 10 for men, and 10 for both sexes. The examiner analyzes of the applicant's prevailing emotional tone, identification with the characters and the level of conflicts and defenses offered. The TAT permits, among other things, insight into the individual's self-image, relative strengths and various needs.

The Personality Assessment Inventory (PAI)

The PAI was developed as a multidimensional alternative to the MMPI for assessing abnormal personality traits. Therefore, the likelihood of encountering this test in the psychological testing process is high.

The test consists of a 344 item questionnaire. The clinical scales may reveal traits such as anxiety, anxiety-related disorders, depression, mania, paranoia, schizophrenia, borderline disorders, and antisocial tendencies. Its value in screening potential police officers is that it can focus on very critical issues such as potential for aggression, substance abuse, and unreliability.

Incomplete Sentence Test (Rotter Incomplete Sentences Blank, second edition)

While not as frequently encountered as psychological testing tools, it is used by some test examiners. The RISB is often used as an initial clinical assessment preceding a more detailed assessment of psychological issues arising from an applicant's specific responses.

The test is designed to provide an index of overall adjustment for adult populations. The title accurately reflects the content of the test. The applicant is required to complete sentences for which a stem of one or two words is provided. There are 40 stems which the applicant must complete. The test results yield a numerical score, which is reflective of the applicant's overall adjustment.

Ink-Blot Test (Rorschach)

The inkblot test, as it is classically known, was first described by Herman Rorschach, a Swiss psychiatrist. It is a diagnostic tool most effectively implemented when it is used with other psychological testing instruments and interpreted by an interviewer who is familiar with the broadest aspects of dynamic psychiatry.

The test consists of 10 ink blot patterns of varying shades and colors. The applicant is asked by the examiner, "What might this be?" Using an applied process, the examiner scores each card. The test is effective in assessing an applicant's objectivity, values, and emotional tendencies as well as revealing neuroses, psychosis, character disorders, addictions, and psychosomatic disorders.

Examiner Qualifications

Certainly, you will want to be confident of the skills and qualifications of the individual conducting the test.

There is no national standardization of qualifications. Each agency establishes its own qualifications governed by their state's statutes. However, a common foundation of skill level is provided.

- A qualified professional is commonly defined as a licensed psychologist who has a doctoral degree in psychology; and at least five years in postgraduate work in the diagnosis and treatment of emotional and mental disorders.

A qualified professional will also possess:

- A knowledge of the research literature related to the psychological screening of law enforcement officers
- A thorough, first-hand knowledge of the peace officer's job as performed by the hiring agency
- An understanding of the job-related criteria—the 15 Job Dimensions (see Chapter Twelve).

Confidentiality

The time you spend with a psychologist will require personal interaction. You can be assured that your reports will remain confidential. Psychological test reports are distributed only on a need-to-know basis. The testing process falls under state and federal regulations which govern the distribution of confidential reports.

Appeal Procedures

In the event you are rejected on the basis of the psychological test, you may have recourse. Agencies that have incorporated the psychological test as a segment of their selection process will, in most jurisdictions, have established guidelines for an applicant to repeal the results of the test. Although procedures will vary from one agency to the next, there may be a written procedure on file which advises the applicant of the steps in the appeal process.

Typical Questions and Answers Relating to the Psychological Test

Q: What won't the psychological testing reveal to the examiner?

A: A good psychological examination will not discriminate on the basis of sex, political affiliation, age, ethnic background, or choice of religion.

Q: What can a good psychological examination reveal to the examiner?

A: To understand what a good evaluation may reveal, think in terms of what a close friend or family member may know about you. With some exceptions, a psychologist can reveal certain personality traits about an applicant that only people with a very long and close relationship with the applicant will know. Unfortunately, those people who could enlighten the hiring agency about an applicant are often unwilling to do so. They have an allegiance to the applicant and not to the department.

Q: Will the psychological testing show my lack of communication skills?

A: In some areas, yes, but the hiring agency does not need a psychological tool to measure all areas of communication skills. A written test will identify the ability to interpret the English language and ability to write a coherent report. A background investigation will reveal indicators of a learning ability by revealing school grades and previous job evaluations. The real value of the psychological testing lies in its ability to predict how the applicant will get along with other people, fellow officers, supervisors, and the public.

Q: Just how accurate is the testing?

A: More so than if none is utilized! In some disciplines, accuracy is estimated to be between 40 and 60 percent.

Q: If I am in a protected class under ADA, how does this test apply?

A: ADA is very clear. By law, employers generally cannot screen for mental disorders that have been diagnosed as a disability. However, it must be reiterated that law enforcement has the necessity to test in order to determine if a person has the capability to perform essential job functions.

Q: Can psychological testing be conducted before a conditional offer of employment is made?

A: The prevailing view held by most law enforcement agencies is that it can. Just as the required physical fitness test is a job-related provision, the psychological evaluation process is as well. The outcome of this testing is part-in-parcel to the total selection process.

In 1986, the International Association of Chiefs of Police, Psychological Services Section mandated guidelines for pre-employment screening. The IACP and the Psychological Services Unit maintain that pre-employment psychological testing should be used as one component of the overall selection process and that psychological recommendations should not be used as the sole criteria for a hire/no hire decision.

Remember, psychological examinations (because they are job-related) are conducted for the purpose of identifying the applicants who are not suitable for employment in law enforcement because they possess inappropriate personality traits.

Q: Is it likely that my history of past abuse of alcohol or illegal drug use will be revealed in the psychological testing?

A: Yes. In most instances, these issues are a component of the evaluation process. Certainly, these issues impact the 15 Job Dimensions as noted in Chapter Twelve. The justification for inquiries into these issues is that extensive research has demonstrated a correlation of past substance abuse to future poor performance in a career in law enforcement.

Q: If I have a history of mental illness, will it be included in my psychological evaluation?

A: Yes. Just as past drug addiction is a job-related issue, so is the emotional and mental stability of the applicant. However, a history of mental health problems is not automatically grounds for rejection. Other factors that might affect the individuals suitability for the position must be considered.

Chapter Eleven

POLYGRAPH EXAMINATION

If you have been scheduled to take a polygraph examination (lie detector test), you are nearing the end of the selection process and are about to embark on a career in law enforcement.

Lawful Authority

The polygraph examination another component of the total hiring process. Its use is widespread, and its legality has been upheld in the higher courts. In *Woodland vs. City of Houston*, the U.S. Court of Appeals for the Fifth Circuit ruled that the constitutionality of pre-employment polygraph testing depends on a balancing of the police department's interests in pre-employment testing and the applicant's privacy interest. In *Anderson vs. The City of Philadelphia*, the U.S. Court of Appeals for the Third Circuit upheld the constitutionality of pre-employment polygraph testing by concluding that it is not " . . . irrational to believe that the polygraph has utility in connection with the selection of law enforcement officers." It also concluded, ". . . reasonable law enforcement administrators may choose to include a polygraph requirement in their hiring process without offending the equal protection clause."

The Examiner

Polygraph operators are professionals in a very unique field. Yet, polygraphy has never received scientific acceptance. It is an art as much as it is a science. Standardization of polygraphy has led to training in a classroom for up to two months. The American Polygraph Association (APA) requires completion of a certified school.

The Test

It is important to remember that all 50 states have developed regulations, statutes, or administrative procedures governing the applicability of polygraph examinations. As they may differ, a broad and general explanation is provided. Specific applications of polygraphs should be verified with the hiring agency.

Most agencies have created a system for pre-employment polygraph testing that focuses the entire examination on the 15 job dimensions (as described in Chapter 12). They will have compiled a battery of nondiscriminatory, job-related, pretest questions that comply with the American Disabilities Act of 1990 (ADA) regulations.

You are encouraged to get a good night's rest before the examination. Being well rested will lower your level of anxiety and nervousness. Plan on at least two hours for the entire test. Wear comfortable clothing, as you will be seated for the majority of the test. You will be seated, facing a blank wall to minimize distraction. A blood pressure-type cuff will be attached around your left arm. The examiner will place two electrodes on fingertips of your right hand, and two corrugated rubberized bellows will be placed across your upper abdomen and chest. Before the test is initiated, the examiner will explain the process in detail. The most important thing is to be completely truthful with the examiner, especially about any possible problems in your past. Law enforcement agencies are not necessarily looking for the person who has made the fewest mistakes in life. Given a choice between one applicant who has made some memorable mistakes, but who has changed his/her ways and an applicant whose mistakes were trivial, but who tried to lie about them or cover them up, most departments will feel more comfortable with the applicant with the colorful past.

Most people are nervous when they are scheduled for a job interview. When that interview is referred to as a lie detector test, the level of anxiety can increase dramatically. To minimize anxiety, answers to some common questions are provided below.

Everything You Wanted to know About Polygraphs, But Were Afraid to Ask

Q: Why do so many law enforcement agencies ask applicants to take a polygraph test?

A: Given the circumstances of today's world, agencies want to hire only those people who meet the high standards that the public expects. They want their community to be served by officers who are well-trained, highly professional, and whose word can be trusted without question. You will be proud to be part of a department that has such high standards, and you have the security of knowing that you will be working with people you can depend on.

Q: I tend to be a nervous person. Even though I am telling the truth, will my nervousness make it seem as though I am lying?

A : Everyone who takes a polygraph test is nervous, and yet most people pass with flying colors. The test process easily compensates for such factors. The examiner will explain this in more detail during your interview. If you have a particular concern about your specific situation, bring this to the attention of the examiner.

Q: I am not exactly a perfect person. How can I pass a lie detector test?

A: People often worry that some negative factor in their past (e.g., a drunk driving arrest, having been fired from a job) will automatically disqualify them from the job. This is not the case. These events are evaluated in the context of the applicant's overall background, rather than as isolated events. Some of the factors that the department will consider are the length of time since the incident, how many times it occurred, and conduct since the last incident. With most departments, the applicant will be allowed to fill out a questionnaire that will identify any potential problems prior to testing. Concerns can be discussed during the interview with the examiner. It is understood that many situations need explanation beyond a simple "yes" or "no."

Q: What kind of questions will I be asked?

A: Polygraph examiners are professionals. You will not be asked any trick or surprise questions. Every question will be read to you, word for word, before the actual test. The scope of the test is limited to finding out whether you are qualified for a job in law enforcement. Some of the areas that are covered are honesty, dependability, ability to function under stress and decision-making ability. You will not be asked embarrassing or personal questions (i.e., political or religious beliefs). You will be asked questions about commission of crimes, including sexual crimes, but you will not be asked about personal activities which are not criminal in nature.

Q: I must admit that I have experimented with drugs. Will that mean that I could fail the test?

A: Drugs are common in today's world. It is realized that law enforcement applicants have not been living in a vacuum. The fact is, most people who are applying for law enforcement jobs have used some type of illegal drugs, and such drug use is not automatically disqualifying. During the interview, the examiner will clarify the extent of your use and the time frame in which it occurred. You will not be expected to remember exact dates or numbers. You will be required to give honest estimates of a number or range that you feel is accurate in answering particular questions. The test questions will verify that you have not deliberately lied bout your drug use. Once again, you should be aware that if you lie about the extent of your drug use, even if that use is quite small, you will have a difficult time gaining acceptance by any law enforcement agency.

Q: How does the polygraph instrument work?

A: The polygraph is a delicately engineered, very sensitive recording device. It records changes that occur in your body, and the examiner has the professional training and skill to interpret these tracings. It is very important to sit still and follow the examiner's directions during the test.

Q: Will the test be painful?

A : No. Your blood pressure is measured in much the same manner as in your doctor's office. The other attachments do not produce any particular sensation, and there is no way the instrument can injure you.

Q: Does the examiner decide whether or not I get the job?

A: No. This decision is made by the hiring authority. The purpose of the polygraph test is to provide the department with information that is used as one part of the selection process.

Q: I think I left something out when I filled out my background forms. What should I do?

A: This happens from time to time. During your interview, make sure that you point out the differences between what you now recall and the information you gave the department in the past. The best policy is to mention the discrepancy at the beginning of the interview, even before you are asked any questions in that area.

Q: Who will get the results of the test?

A: The results of the test are highly confidential. The report will normally be routed to the assigned background investigator. It is his/her responsibility to maintain the confidential nature of the report.

Information Resources

Central Coast Polygraph
FBI Law Enforcement Bulletin, November, 1993.

Chapter Twelve

BACKGROUND INVESTIGATION

A re you ready for the scrutiny of a background investigation? As a viable police candidate, you will participate in the background investigation process. It is inevitable. There once was a day when you as a new officer met with the chief, he put a badge on your chest, a gun on your hip, gave you the keys to a patrol car and put you on the streets. Those days are gone.

Civil liability has forced law enforcement to seek out only the most qualified personnel. The public has a right to have only the highest character of officer on its police forces. As agencies look for only the best, an intricate stage in that process is the background investigation.

As you will soon see, the fundamental characteristic that agencies look for is honesty, and determining honesty requires a long, in-depth investigation. Dishonesty in the selection pool does exist and accounts for a significant percentage of potential candidates who are rejected from the testing process. An illustration of how this common dishonesty is found is in the results of a study on cheating at a reputable Midwestern university. This study revealed that 91 percent of the students admitted to having cheated at least once during their undergraduate studies. Clearly, it would be senseless to think police officials would reject 91 percent of available candidates and only select from the 9 percent pool of students who did not cheat. Law enforcement understands that young people make mistakes, but they are not so understanding as to consider a candidate who graduated by relying on fraudulent accomplishments. It is important to understand that police executives do not expect applicants to be beyond reproach in their personal histories. However, there are limits to acceptable past transgressions (which is the essence of the following 15 job dimensions). These criteria are accepted systematic tools used in the background selection process. For most agencies, subjective analysis, which can include prejudice, bias and racism, is minimized. In its place is a set of criteria that is used to assist in determining whether a candidate's background is acceptable.

Job Dimensions

Law enforcement agencies have a moral and ethical obligation to select only the best qualified candidates for employment. The obligation also carries a legal responsibility to ensure that all applicants are treated equally and fairly. In meeting these challenges, agencies recognize that certain duties and responsibilities are necessary dimensions of law enforcement. Those dimensions are:

1) Communication skills—Ability to express oneself verbally and in writing. Ability to read with good comprehension. Ability to write a report which accurately describes what has occurred. Ability to speak clearly and make oneself understood.

2) Problem solving ability—Ability to "size-up" a situation, identify the problem(s), and make a logical decision. Ability to compare and contrast situations confronted on a daily basis. Using good judgement in making decisions.

3) Learning ability—Ability to comprehend, retain and recall factual information pertaining to laws, statutes, codes, etc. Ability to learn and apply what is learned.

4) Judgment under pressure—Apply good common sense when dealing with high pressure situations. Ability to make sound on-the-spot decisions.

5) Observational skills—Mental alertness, memory for details. Alert to signals which indicate that something might be wrong. Suspicious and inquisitive.

6) Willingness to confront a problem—Ability to be assertive in a potentially explosive situation. Willingness to confront a problem and not back away. Courage to attend to a potentially dangerous situation.

7) Interest in people—Desire to understand and work with people. Non-prejudice.

8) Interpersonal sensitivity—Resolve problems in sensitive manner. Show empathy. Effectiveness in dealing with people and understanding their motives.

9) Desire for self-improvement—Desire to seek the knowledge needed to become a confident law enforcement officer. Seeing oneself as being responsible for learning the job. Having a high degree of motivation and desire to improve skills and knowledge.

10) Appearance—Having personal and professional pride in one's demeanor and appearance.

11) Dependability—Submitting reports in a timely manner. Motivated. Expends extra effort to be accurate in all details. Willingness to put in extra hours to complete a job.

12) Physical ability—Physical endurance to do the job well.

13) Integrity and honesty—Refusing to yield to the temptations of bribes, gratuities, etc. Refusing to tolerate unethical and illegal conduct on the part of other law enforcement personnel. Strong moral character.

14) Operation of a motor vehicle—Ability to drive safely at high speeds and in all types of conditions.

15) Credibility as a witness in a court of law—Ability to testify in a court of law without being subject to impeachment due to character flaws, past harmful acts, or prior felony conviction.

Provided is detailed information that will explain and break down the typical background investigation used by most law enforcement agencies. Review the above 15 job dimensions. As you learn more about the purpose of the background investigation, personal history statement, and interview, you will understand how your personal history may conflict with aspects of the 15 job dimensions in ways that will *not* be considered acceptable. If a candidate fails to meet all of the 15 job dimensions, he/she may fail to meet the standards of a successful background investigation.

What Is The Agency's Goal?

In simplistic terms, the background investigation is designed to determine whether an applicant meets the minimum requirements, and possesses the moral character, to perform the duties of a law enforcement officer. Background investigations will delve into the applicant's history, seeking insight regarding:

- *Attitude:*

  A position assumed, indicative of a positive mood or condition; state of mind or feeling with regard to a person or thing.

- *Motivation:*

  That within an individual that invites him/her to action; **commitment**.

- *Stability*:

  Long-lasting and enduring; emotionally well balanced and sound; **dependable.**

- *Aptitude*:

  Natural talent, quickness in learning; **suitability**.

- *Demeanor:*

  Outward bearing, behavior, manners; **command presence**.

- *Maturity:*

  Having reached full growth or development; **responsible**.

The purpose of the background investigation is more than determining the applicant's physical qualifications, writing skills, reading level, etc. Investigators want to know what you have succeeded in, in the past; how you handle failure; how others perceive you; and behavior that might reveal:

- Questionable integrity
- Lack of dependability
- Poor credibility
- Inability to handle stress

These traits may be revealed in discrepancies, factual omissions and intentional misrepresentations, all of which are concerns which cannot be ignored.

C.A.R.L's 4 P's

C Character. Moral fortitude. Honesty.

A Association. With peers and/or colleagues.

R Relatives. Stability. Support.

L Loyalty. Commitment. Service.

P = People
Relatives, co-workers, former spouses, teachers, friends and the candidate him/herself.

P = Paper
Personal history statement, birth certificate, marriage license, divorce decree, civil suits, employment applications, etc.

P = Personal Observation
Body language, demeanor, verbal expression, writing skills, compliance with directions.

P = Polygraph
Technology and instrument to reveal truth; not an arbitrary judgment.

What Can You Do To Prepare?

Take the time to prepare for the process and avoid critical pitfalls. Show the investigator that you will be an asset to the organization. Follow each directive thoroughly and in a timely manner. Prepare every document you are asked to complete in a professional manner. A personal history statement with poor penmanship, grammatical and spelling errors and omissions will set the stage for a negative evaluation.

Know in advance that relatives, former and current employers, friends and co-workers will be contacted for their opinion as to whether you will make a suitable law enforcement officer. Inform them in advance, and assure them that they are to speak freely with the background investigator.

Subjecting the applicant to the third degree is not interviewing!

There is a difference between an interview and an interrogation. Keep this interview in perspective. You are not in custody! The investigator's job is to establish a rapport that is conducive to effective communication.

The quality and quantity of information that the background investigator obtains will depend on his/her ability to formulate and ask pertinent questions.

Untruthfulness will be in the back of every background investigator's mind. If an applicant attempts to hide, minimize or falsify any information, that applicant risks rejection. The background investigator will be keen to body language consistent with deception.

If you lie, they will let you lie, and then they will write it down.

Failure to maintain eye contact, exhibiting nervous fidgeting, and displaying posture with crossed arms and legs may indicate deception. Speech patterns, voice clarity and affect are also noted carefully.

If an applicant includes a question, either to the interviewer or someone else, in his/her response, the interviewer will wonder why.

Personal History Statement

As your background investigation begins, you will be provided with a packet, varying from five to 15 pages. This packet is referred to as the *personal history statement*. The personal history statement contains questions regarding most areas of an applicant's life. The personal history statement was developed to help the investigator focus on those areas of inquiry which have the greatest potential for yielding job-related information.

You will probably notice that some traditionally used personal history aspects are excluded. Certain subject matters are excluded in response to legal guidelines pursuant to statutory and/or case law. Yet, many of these off-limit issues are more appropriately addressed in other components of the selection process. *Example:* The issue of job-relevant physical defects should be addressed in the medical examination, not the background investigation.

Attachments

Have available a copy of all of the documents the investigator will request. Come prepared! These items will include:

- Driver's license
- Proof of automobile insurance
- College transcripts
- College degree
- Social security card
- High school diploma
- Birth certificate

- Marriage license(s)

- Divorce decree(s)

- Citizenship papers

- Current credit report

- Current photo

(Note: Most departments will not require a photograph, but will accept photos if voluntarily offered.)

If you do not have certain documents immediately available, you risk delaying completion of the investigation. Request copies of the needed documents prior to the interview. These items may be retrieved from the Department of Motor Vehicles, County Clerk, Bureau of Vital Statistics, etc.

Read the directions carefully on the personal history statement. The agency may require that certain documents be official copies, notarized, etc. If you are testing for more than one agency, insure that all of your answers on the personal history statement are truthful and consistent. Law enforcement background investigators have developed a network of communication between agencies. As a matter of routine, a background investigator will contact surrounding law enforcement agencies to see if other agencies have started or completed a background investigation. If they have, that report will be obtained. The information you include on your personal history statement will be compared to those written for other agencies. If inconsistencies exist, you have a problem!

The Interview

Be assured that the investigator has prepared for the interview. Uncertain issues or unverified information will certainly be addressed. A list of questions will have been prepared. Remember, the interview is the primary investigative tool of the background investigator.

The first task of the interviewer is to make the applicant feel comfortable.

The investigator is trained to let the applicant make his/her statement and tell his/her story without being judgmental or critical. If by accident, you note an unintentional error in any part of the personal history statement or application, bring this to his/her attention and correct the error. *Feedback is welcomed!*

The interviewer will strive to develop trust and confidence so you will feel comfortable requesting and offering feedback. If done correctly, feedback will verify that what has been heard has been correctly understood.

Upon conclusion of the interview, comply with any requests made to you. Follow through immediately. Request a business card and ask permission to call back at a later date to determine if there are any further requests. If you should move or change telephone numbers, it is your responsibility to notify the investigator.

Do not call and ask, "Did I pass?"

The rules of confidentiality are rigid and are on a need-to-know basis. The background investigator's responsibility is to conduct the investigation and forward the findings to the hiring authority. If concerns have arisen, they will be clarified in detail in the final report. In the event of a discrepancy or contradiction, the investigator will schedule a second interview. This discrepancy interview will provide an opportunity for the applicant to explain or correct these inconsistencies. In most cases, the background investigator is not asked to make a recommendation of whether or not to hire the applicant. The background investigator's report will be a component of the overall process of selection.

If you fail to meet one or more of the 15 job dimensions, the report will identify these with detailed explanations. Any decision to reject a candidate based on the background investigation will occur at the hiring authority level.

AMERICAN DISABILITIES ACT of 1990

The topic of ADA is sufficiently covered in Chapter 9. However, it is important to briefly cover this subject as it applies to the personal history statement.

With reference to the background process, certain pre-employment inquiries are prohibited if they are asked *prior to a conditional offer of employment*. Those inquiries include questions regarding an applicants' physical or mental disability, history of illness, or any question regarding worker's compensation history. If the background investigation is conducted *after* a conditional job offer is made, these prohibitions *do not* apply.

Confidentiality

The information given by the applicant in the personal history statement and information obtained by the investigator is private and confidential. At no time during the investigation should any information be revealed to persons other than those authorized to receive the results. As a general rule, information gathered from third persons during the background investigation will not be revealed to the applicant.

Release of Information

You will be requested to sign a Release of Information form. Your background investigator will be contacting individuals who will provide information regarding your past. For the protection of the hiring agency, and the investigator himself, as well as neighbors, references, former employers, etc., a release of information form is **required.** *Note: You may be asked to have your signature notarized.*

Contents

The personal history statement will cover a variety of subjects.

• Personal	• Employment
• Relatives	• Military
• References	• Financial
• Education	•Criminal History
• Residence	•Motor Vehicle Operation

- **Personal.** Personal information is requested for the purpose of verifying that the applicant is who he/she claims to be. The verification process will include personal identifiers such as:

  √ Name, addresses, phone numbers, birth date, etc.

  √ Citizenship status

  √ Social security number

  √ Height, weight, eye color, hair color

  √ Scars, tattoos, or other distinguishing marks

  √ AKA (also known as). *Note:* If you have used any other names, be sure to include them. A successful criminal history search depends on utilizing all known identifiers. *Of course, if you have used other identities for illegal purposes, you probably need not read further!*

The use of religious or ancestral names, the decision of a woman *not* to use her husband's last name, or the decision of a man to *use* his wife's last name is not considered improper. The law permits individuals to use any name as long as the change of name is not for fraudulent purposes.

- **Relatives and References.** Your personal history statement will ask for names of friends, relatives, co-workers, roommates, references, etc. Simply put, the background investigator will understand that anyone who knows the applicant is a potential source of job-relevant information. The investigator will contact many potential sources, including school authorities, past landlords, military commanding officers and acquaintances with whom you may have lost touch.

  These contacts further represent potential sources for secondary references. That is, they might be able to supply names of other individuals who may have knowledge of the applicant. Many times, such secondary references prove to be more candid than primary references supplied by the applicant.

  Family members are consulted to determine the applicants ability or willingness to confront problems, his/her level of interest in people, interpersonal sensitivity, dependability and integrity.

An applicant with a history of dysfunctional family problems, serious interpersonal deficiencies, chronic or severe marital problems, or problems associated with physical or psychological abuse may have difficulty in coping with the day-in and day-out duties of a police officer. This is not to imply that the background investigator will be invading your family's personal privacy. The investigator will not seek to uncover every minor family disagreement and dispute. Rather, inquiry will be limited to determine the severity of a significant dysfunction and ensure that it will not affect job performance.

- **Spousal Interview.** Many times, the investigator will schedule an interview with the applicant's spouse. This interview *should* be in the presence of the applicant and conducted in the applicant's residence. It is important that the spouse be given an opportunity to express his/her opinion about a career in law enforcement. Offering opinions, clarifying expectations and communicating concerns are vital to the applicant's success in law enforcement and also to the stability of the marriage. It is *essential* that an applicant discuss his/her goals with his/her spouse *before* acceptance of employment. Absolute understanding on the part of both parties is vital before the applicant puts on a badge. The spousal interview will provide a vehicle for the spouse to ask pertinent questions that may have not yet been addressed

- **Prior Spouse(s).** Although it may cause an applicant discomfort, a prior spouse may have information which reflects upon the applicant's integrity, willingness to confront problems, and interpersonal sensitivity. Expect the investigator to interview all prior spouses. The possibility of negative comments based on emotional anger or resentment will be taken into consideration and balanced by factual corroboration.

- **Education.** Educational minimum requirements must be verified. If you met the requirement of the General Education Development (GED) exam, the acceptable score will be confirmed. Beyond the obvious, inquiries into the applicant's educational background can lead to information concerning integrity, learning ability and desire for self-improvement. Once again, these are components of the 15 job dimensions.

Contacts will include high school teachers, coaches and administrators. Factors of interest include extra curricular activities, clubs, achievements, scholarships, etc. Negative activities will also be investigated. Inquiries into expulsions and/ or suspensions will be made.

Undergraduate studies are also researched. What core courses you have taken, your major of choice, and your grade point average (GPA) are of interest. If the agency requires a college degree, the investigator will determine whether the institution is an accredited college or university. Caution should be exercised. If the agency requires course work from an accredited institution, and you have graduated from, or are attending, one that is not, you may have invested a great deal of time and money needlessly.

- *Residence.* You will be asked to provide a detailed list of past residences. Time frames for residential history vary from agency to agency. Generally, most law enforcement agencies will research 10 to 15 years into the past.

Former neighbors, landlords and apartment managers can offer information regarding the applicant's character. If there appears to be a pattern of frequent moves, failure to pay rent on time, or evictions, this may cause concern. Residential patterns can be indicative of stability, financial responsibility and ability to get along with people.

- *Employment.* The investigation into the applicant's employment history is generally one of the most informative in the background investigation. Dependability and integrity, two of the 15 job dimensions, will surface as the investigation unfolds.

Typically, you will be required to list all jobs held in the past 10 to 15 years. *All* jobs are to be listed, including part-time positions. You may not see the importance of a part-time job held years ago, but omitting it could be viewed as intentional deception. In addition to listing all jobs, be sure to include all periods of military service and unemployment as well. *Do not* leave it up to the background investigator to piece together your work-related history. Let the investigator determine whether it is relevant. You will be asked to list how long these jobs were held and the reasons you left. Do not exaggerate the length of time you worked. Each employer will be confirmed by the background investigator.

Reasons for leaving a position must be carefully and accurately articulated. Your former employer, co-workers and personnel records are going to be utilized as verification. A vague explanation for a past termination may be all that is needed to disqualify you from further consideration. Rejection may not necessarily be based on a specific reason for termination, but rather on the premise that you misled the background investigator. There are very few allowances made when it comes to absolute truthfulness (integrity), especially regarding work history, no matter how inconsequential.

As you are asked to explain your previous jobs, do so thoroughly. Do not sell yourself short. Explain, in detail, your experiences, skills and accomplishments. If necessary, use an additional 8 1/2" x 11" sheet of paper. Be sure to list all titles you held, accomplishments, promotions and special assignments.

Explain only extended or frequent periods of unemployment in detail. Periods of unemployment may be the result of full-time school, work injury, personal or family crisis, etc. If you have been in receipt of welfare assistance or unemployment compensation, indicate this. Receipt of such benefits is legal and will not be judged negatively.

• *Military.* Your military experience may have provided you with valuable knowledge, training and experience. Formalized training, practical vocational application and military discipline are valuable assets to any police organization. From a background investigation standpoint, it can address #13 (Integrity) of the 15 job dimensions. Military training is demanding. Moral fortitude, commitment and loyalty are important character traits to any police organization.

The personal history statement will ask for the branch of service, service number, dates of service and type of discharge. Of particular concern to the investigator will be the type of discharge. A discharge of anything less than honorable will require a thorough explanation. Your DD-214 will list the type of discharge granted.

If you were disciplined (Article 15, Title 15), be prepared to explain in detail the nature of this action. The adjudication of judicial or nonjudicial military disciplinary actions may reflect upon your integrity, dependability or judgment under pressure.

If no military service is reported, verification will be obtained ensuring that you are in compliance with Selective Service registration requirements.

- *Financial.* An applicant's handling of financial affairs can reflect integrity, problem-solving ability, and dependability. The personal history statement will request a complete account of current assets and liabilities and a statement of current income and expenditures. You will asked to list all debts, repossessions, tax liens, charge accounts, contracts and any financial liability.

  Bankruptcy. If you have filed for Chapter 7, Chapter 11, or Chapter 13, under the U.S. Bankruptcy Code, a full and complete disclosure will be requested. Unpaid bills turned over to a collection agency may reflect an applicant's integrity, problem-solving ability or dependability.

  Repossession. Overspending or falsifying, resulting in the purchased goods being repossessed, is a concern to the investigation.

  Wages Garnished. If a debtor went to the effort to garnish wages, the reason is surely significant and will require an explanation.

  Delinquent Taxes. Information regarding delinquent federal income taxes or other tax payments, would generally not be used to disqualify you, unless there is indication of intent to defraud.

  Credit Report. A law enforcement officer must be financially responsible. The frequency of an applicant's rejection due, in part, to an unsuitable credit history is alarming. Whether the hiring agency requests one from you or they obtain one themselves, a current credit report will be acquired. You are encouraged to get a report for your own records. Credit reporting agencies are notorious for inaccurate records. Should this occur, it is best to resolve the issue before the background investigation commences.

  In accordance with federal law, accurate information, such as late payments or an account turned over to a collection agency, can remain on your credit record for seven years. However, Chapter 7, 11, and 12 bankruptcies can remain on your credit report for up to 10 years. (A Chapter 13 bankruptcy remains on your credit report for seven years from the date it was filed.)

By obtaining your credit record in advance, you can resolve any disputes before the background investigator asks you about them. Credit reporting agencies are known for disbursing inaccurate records. If you have a dispute regarding an entry, place your concern in writing and send it to the reporting agency. Upon receipt, they will contact the parties involved and conduct the necessary assessment. An adjustment to your credit report will be made if justified. In most cases, this process takes about 30 days.

If a poor credit history is legitimate, be ready to explain each and every entry to the background investigator. There is nothing you can do about the past. Be truthful and candid when asked to explain.

- *Civil Suits.* The background investigator will need to know of any involvement in civil court actions and whether you were the plaintiff or defendant. Investigations into past civil actions may have a direct parallel to #15 (Credibility as a witness in a court of law) of the 15 job dimensions. If you had a civil judgment against you, the cause is clearly relevant. Dependability, responsibility and integrity are all related matters that may impact your background investigation. Regardless of outcome, come prepared with a copy of the court action and make it available to the investigator.

- *Criminal History.* As your background investigation commences, you will have provided several sources of personal identification. You will also be fingerprinted. With these, a thorough nationwide search will commence to determine the extent of your criminal history. Criminal repositories that will be contacted include the Federal Bureau of Investigation (FBI), State Criminal History Repository, and local city, county, and state references.

Each jurisdiction has its own standards of acceptable behavior and past criminal history. In the event you have a criminal record, you are encouraged to contact the hiring authority before you test to ensure you meet their qualifications.

- *Felony Convictions.* If you are a convicted felon, you will *not* qualify for a job in law enforcement. There are rare and conditional exceptions to this rule. For specific questions, contact the specific hiring agency to which you are applying.

- *Misdemeanor Convictions.* There is a wide difference of standards across the nation as to the acceptance of past misdemeanor convictions. This criteria has a direct correlation with #13 (integrity) and #15 (credibility as a witness in a court of law) of the 15 job dimensions. Agencies will take into consideration the severity of offense and the degree of severity, time elapsed since offense and the degree of sanction imposed.

It is not possible to identify minimum standards used by law enforcement agencies. At best, a random set of examples that are typically considered unacceptable criminal history are provided:

- Any misdemeanor conviction involving crimes of moral turpitude

- Any misdemeanor property crime involving larceny, concealment, bad checks, embezzlement

- Any conviction of perjury

- Any conviction involving crimes of violence

- Any conviction involving sex crimes

- Any conviction involving domestic violence

- Numerous arrests or convictions for misdemeanors or crimes of a more serious nature

- Any misdemeanor conviction, regardless how minor, within 12 months preceding the date of application

- Any conviction for driving under the influence (DWI and/or DUI) within three years preceding the date of application

- ***Domestic Violence Conviction.*** On September 30, 1996, the parameters for hiring law enforcement personnel with prior convictions involving domestic violence revolutionalized the selection process. The United States Congress passed the Omnibus Consolidated Appropriations Act of 1997, inclusive of an amendment to the Federal Gun Control Act (GCA).

In layman's terms, the law forbids any person convicted of an encompassed offense from ever possessing a firearm or ammunition, including law enforcement officers. Congress provided no allowances, exceptions or time frame under the statutes. To summarize the scope of this law, an applicant cannot be considered for employment if ever having been convicted of a crime of violence, the attempted crime of violence or the implied use of a deadly weapon against:

√ A spouse

√ An ex-spouse

√ A parental party

√ A person whom the victim and the perpetrator had a child in common

√ Adult guardian of the victim

√ A person cohabiting with the victim as a spouse, parent or guardian

√ A person who formerly cohabitated as a spouse, parent or guardian

√ A person similarly situated to a spouse, parent or guardian of the victim

The impact of this law has had a significant role on the hiring process for all law enforcement agencies across the country. Until this law was enacted, a candidate wasn't necessarily rejected from further consideration due to a misdemeanor conviction of this nature. The hiring authority had the discretion to take the factors surrounding the circumstances of the conviction into account. Extenuating circumstances may have precipitated the event and consideration may be given to how the applicant has ameliorated his/her life-style since the conviction. Discretion allows the agency to take into account:

AMENDMENTS TO THE FEDERAL GUN CONTROL ACT OF 1968

MADE BY THE OMNIBUS CONSOLIDATED APPROPRIATIONS LAW OF 1997

90 PUBLIC LAW 104-208, TITLE 18, UNITED STATES CODE, SECTION 922 (d)(9) and (g)(9)

18 USC 922 (d)(9) "It shall be unlawful for any person to sell, or otherwise dispose of, any firearm or ammunition to any person knowing or having reasonable cause to believe that such a person . . .has been convicted in any court of a misdemeanor crime of domestic violence."

18 USC 922 (g) (9) "It shall be unlawful for any person . . . who has been convicted in any court of a misdemeanor crime of domestic violence, or to ship or transport in interstate or foreign commerce, or possess in or affecting commerce, any firearm or ammunition; or to receive any firearm or ammunition which has been shipped or transported in interstate foreign commerce."

18 USC 921 (a)(33)(A) "Except as provided in subparagraph (C), the term misdemeanor crime of 'domestic violence' means an offense the. . . (j) is a misdemeanor under state or federal law; and . . .(ii) has, as an element, the use or attempted use of physical force, or the threatened use of a deadly weapon, committed by a current or former spouse, parent, or guardian of the victim , by a person with whom the victim shares a child in common, by a person who is cohabiting with or has cohabited with the victim as a spouse, parent or guardian of the victim."

(B) (I) A person shall not be considered to have been convicted of such an offense for purposes of this chapter, unless . . . (I) the person was represented by counsel in the case, or knowingly and intelligently waived the right to counsel in the case, and; (II) in the case of a prosecution for an offense described in this paragraph for which a person was entitled to a jury trial in the jurisdiction in which the case was tried, either (aa) the case was tried by a jury or (bb) the person knowingly and intelligently waived the right to have the case tried by a jury, by guilty plea or otherwise.

(ii) A person shall not be considered to be convicted of such an offense for the purposes of this chapter if the conviction has been expunged or set aside, or is an offense for which the person has been pardoned or had civil rights restored (if the law of the applicable jurisdiction provides for the loss of civil rights under such an offense) unless the pardon, expungement, or restoration of civil rights expressly provides that the person may not ship, transport, possess, or receive firearms."

√ Whether it was a one-time event

√ The age of the applicant at the time of the offense

√ The nature of the offense

√ The severity of the offense

√ Time frame since occurence

√ Remorsefulness

√ Therapeutic intervention

Every applicant who is impacted by this law must assess his/ her own situation to determine if he/she will be excluded on the basis of this law. It would be prudent for the applicant to review the applicable statutes of the jurisdiction where the conviction occurred. Legal advice is certainly encouraged. Misdemeanor laws pertaining to domestic violence vary from state to state. Congress was careful to incorporate provisions into the law for those persons not prohibited from carrying or possessing a firearm or ammunition. The law is not applicable if the applicant's conviction has been expunged (erased), set aside, or has been pardoned or has had civil rights restored (if the law of the applicable jurisdiction provides for the loss of civil rights under such an offense) and unless the restoration of civil rights specifically permitted the right to bear arms.

- *Juvenile Offenses.* The philosophy of juvenile law is that juveniles are not arrested or convicted of crimes in the adult sense. However, if the applicant committed an offense as a juvenile that would have been a crime had he/she been an adult, that information may be relevant to the background investigator for assessing integrity, dependability, or credibility of the witness in a court of law once the facts and circumstances have been ascertained. If the juvenile was treated as an adult and convicted of a felony, the applicant *cannot* be a police officer.

- *Motor Vehicle Operation.* The ability to safely operate a motor vehicle in the performance of a peace officer's duties is essential. Therefore, it was deemed important enough to include this subject as one of the 15 job dimensions. For this reason, a candidate's driving record will be carefully reviewed. If you possess a valid driver's license with no traffic violations, there will be no problem. If you have a history of repeated moving violations, serious traffic violations (i.e., reckless driving, speed contests, etc.), license revocations and/or suspensions, you may encounter difficulty passing a background investigation.

Once again, it is not possible to provide a set of acceptable standards regarding motor vehicle violations. Evaluating an applicant's driving record is very subjective. If there are concerns, an applicant should contact the individual hiring agency.

- *General Topics.* Background investigators will conduct investigations into many different areas which apply to the applicant's suitability for employment.

  - Illegal drug use.

  - Subversive activity. If you have ever participated in or belonged to a subversive group dedicated to the overthrow of the U.S. government, you will not meet the standards of a successful background investigation.

  - Insurance. An investigator may inquire into whether an applicant ever had insurance (e.g., health, life, etc.) refused or canceled (for reasons other than failure to pay premiums). Such information may reflect upon his/her integrity or physical ability.

  - Permit to carry a concealed weapon. You may be asked in the personal history statement if you have ever applied for or received a permit to carry a concealed weapon. Although this is not a legal concern, it is a justifiable one. The reasons for such a request should be clearly explained.

  - Other Police Officer Testing. It is not uncommon for an applicant to test simultaneously with multiple agencies. No one will fault an applicant for these efforts. It is not uncommon for agencies to compete with each other to expedite the selection process in order to be the first to offer a position to the best applicants.

Consequently, you may have multiple background investigations being conducted simultaneously. As noted earlier, background investigators communicate closely with one another and share information. This is why it is so important to be consistent in regards to the information you supply on your application and the personal history statement. Inform the investigator of your testing processes at other agencies and provide them with a release of information so the necessary contacts can be made.

- Sexual, Political and Religious Behavior. No routine inquiry should be made into the applicant's *legal* sexual, political, or religious behavior. Such behavior itself is *not* job-related.

Chapter Thirteen

THE CHOICE IS MADE

Y ou have made a choice, to pursue a career in law enforcement. The profession is demanding, requiring unconditional loyalty and commitment. Few occupations demand such intensive scrutiny during the hiring process, and yet you've chosen to go forward to participate in the selection process. You won't be alone. The competition will be intense. You may be vying with hundreds, even thousands, of applicants trying to fill a handful of vacancies. Statistically, for every officer hired, there are 250 unsuccessful applicants. What determines the successful applicant and those that fail? Preparation. Preparation is where a successful candidate separates himself/herself from the others.

There are no shortcuts and no gimmicks to being chosen as the number one applicant. Mastering the principles of preparation and applying your energy are the only ways you will achieve the desired goals you seek. This book's intent is designed to provide a framework for preparation and a blueprint of knowledge for the applicant preparing to participate in the entire testing process. Each testing phase has its own purpose and can be successfully passed with the proper effort and commitment. If the applicant is ill-prepared and fails even one step in the process, that applicant becomes merely a statistic of the unsuitable candidates. Therefore, lets briefly summarize the various steps of the selection process and those criteria that will assist you in reaching your goal.

Application Process: As inconsequential as it may seem, a properly prepared and timely submission of the employment application is as important as any of the other testing stages. The application form must be neat and legible, preferably typed. Ensure that it is filled out in it's entirety. Your application form becomes a reflection of you and your potential as an officer. It is going to be reviewed by the personnel analyst, oral board members and the background investigator. You can't afford to turn in a half-prepared, sloppy application. Lastly, the closing date for receipt of your application must meet the established timeframe. Rarely, will an application be accepted if turned in past the closing date.

Medical/Physical Requirements: Law enforcement officers must be physically prepared to perform all of the strenuous activities they may face in any given tour of duty. A physically unfit officer not only places himself/herself in serious jeopardy but also may risk the safety of the victim who is depending on the officer's protection. The selection process will ensure applicants meet certain physical qualifications. A thorough medical evaluation will be performed inclusive of vision, hearing, respiratory and cardiovascular systems and in some instances, height and weight requirements.

Drug Testing: The necessity for members of any policing agency to be drug free is obvious. Pre-employment drug screening for law enforcement applicants common throughout the United States with all law enforcement agencies. Plan on it. Drug screen testing will look for the presence of any illegal controlled substance and evidence of abuse of legal prescription medications. Inevitably, the issue of past drug use is raised. Will past drug use mean an automatic rejection? No. At one time, any use whatsoever would mean the applicant was unqualified. Times have changed. Law enforcement agencies have established standards regarding past drug use. Standards tend to vary from agency to agency, depending on the type of drug used and the length of time since its use.

Written Examination: The written test will generally be the first test a candidate will take. Written tests vary in content but all are designed to assess an applicant's abilities to follow and understand directions, problem solving, decision-making, memory observation, basic grammar, spelling and writing skills. To be successful on the written test, an applicant must study and thoroughly prepare. Are you willing and motivated to study long hours? This effort is essential to improve on your ability to not only pass the written test but to pass with the highest score among your peers.

Physical Fitness Test: The police recruitment process will require the candidate to pass a physical fitness test. The importance of excelling at this test is no less important than passing the written test with a high score. Preparation for this part of the selection process begins long before the date the test is proctored. The methods used for testing vary greatly around the country. The most popular test is one that utilizes norm-referenced testing, which means each test taker's score is compared to the scores of established referenced tests, inclusive of,

* Cardiorespiratory endurance testing

* Abdominal and lower back strength

* Muscular strength and endurance

* Flexibility

* Body composition or percentage of body fat

If perhaps you have ignored your physical condition and your ability to meet established minimum requirements is in doubt, you can wait no longer to improve your physical condition.

Oral Board: The primary purpose of the oral board interview is to assess an applicant's integrity, initiative, communication skills, tolerance for stress, judgment and decisiveness. It is the applicant's opportunity to show his desire for personal growth, commitment, enthusiasm and his potential value to the hiring agency. How an applicant performs on the oral board begins with the applicant's degree of preparation. The first five minutes of an oral board can set the tone. Practice and rehearsal for the oral presentation can greatly improve one's performance.

Psychological Test: Most law enforcement agencies utilize a variety of testing components to conduct the psychological examination. With these tests, various personality traits are sought. Specific traits considered vital in police work include: logical reasoning, compatibility, self-confidence, diplomacy, stress tolerance, positive motivation and behavioral flexibility. Conversely, test data look for unfavorable traits, such as inability to handle stress, low interpersonal skills, negative emotional control and violent or aggressive behavior.

Polygraph Examination: Use of the polygraph examination is common for entry level testing. Its purpose is quite obvious. You will be questioned as to your honesty on the information you supplied on your initial employment application, oral board presentation and the results of your background investigation. There is nothing to fear about taking a polygraph test, except, of course ,if you try to lie, frivolously mitigate an issue, or intentionally omit any information. So how do you successfully pass the lie detector exam? Simple. Tell the truth.

Law enforcement provides an immensely fulfilling career. I wish you the best of luck in your quest of attaining a position. I trust this book was helpful, and the choice made will be the one you have strived for.

Appendix

WHERE AND HOW TO FIND JOB OPENINGS

So you have reached that point where you are now trying to find which law enforcement agencies are hiring. How do you find that one agency that meets all your expectations? You have spent countless hours of preparation, studying and honing your physical condition. You have discovered, however, that navigating blindly through an employment search by making expensive long distance phone calls and sending out an innumerable amount of letters of interest are resulting in that all to common response, "We're not hiring at this time." Where do you turn?

Twenty, ten and even just five years ago, an aspiring applicant had to rely on newspaper classified ads, letters on interest and resumes and phone calls to learn where and when an agency would be hiring. Times have changed, and so has your ability to learn when and where law enforcement agencies would be seeking entry level officers. The vast amount of information that is available on the world wide web has opened the doors for job seekers to monitor daily those agencies that are in the process of hiring. A number of these sources are provided for your job search efforts.

■ **The Police Officer's Internet Directory**

URL: www.officer.com

Over 1500 individual home pages of information of law enforcement agencies across the country. Included is a state-by-state breakdown of agencies with current openings.

■ **On Patrol**

URL: info@onpatrol.com

Provided are free postings of law enforcement opportunities on a state-by-state basis.

■ Career Path

URL: www.careerpath.com

Career Path is a leading site on the world wide web for job seekers. Powered by the nation's leading newspapers, Career Path offers law enforcement job seekers the greatest number of the most current recruitment efforts by law enforcement agencies. After selecting a geographical location, the applicant can peruse the major newspaper classified ads for current openings for that area.

■ Women Peace Officers Association of California

URL: N/A

This association maintains a current register of California law enforcement agencies recruitment efforts. Mailing address: Women Peace Officers Association, 39525 Los Alamos Road 4 A, Murrieta, CA; (909) 698-6216.

■ Ira Wilsker

URL: iwilsker@ih2OOO.net

A current, state-by-state listing of law enforcement job vacancies for all 50 states.

■ Blue Line Police Opportunity Monitor

URL:www.theblueline.com/publication.htm

The Blue Line is a monthly publication featuring public service jobs and police officer positions across the United States.

■ The Central Organization for Police Selection (COPS)

URL: N/A

COPS is a screening and testing program for law enforcement applicants for 21 cities along the Colorado front range. The applicant determines which jurisdiction may consider his or her application for employment. The examination is given twice a year. Contact: Denver Regional Council of Governments 2480 W. 26 th Ave, Suite. 2OOB, Denver, CO 80211-5580, phone # (303) 455-1000.

■ **FCF Law Enforcement Employment Guides**

URL: www.gate.net/fcfjobs

FCF provides a 37 page employment guide listing of 33 Agent/ Officer federal careers and present openings and a 51 page guide listing of all 50 states' troopers and current hirings. Contact: FCF, P.O. Box 2176, Brunswick, GA, 31521

■ **National Public Safety Institute**

URL: N/A

Provides a law enforcement job finder for vacancies in city, county, state, federal and corporate agencies throughout the United States. Contact: National Public Safety Institute/ Criminal Justice Career Consultants, 2315 N. Casa Granda Ave., Casa Grande, AZ 85230.

■ **Federal Support Service**

URL: N/A

An information guide of listings regarding state police career information and federal law enforcement job openings, job banks and recruitment hotline phone numbers. Contact: Federal Support Service, P.O. Box 742, Tallman, NY 10982.

■ **Federal Services Bureau**

URL: N/A

An information guide and recruitment hotlines for 116 federal law enforcement careers in covert operations, intelligence, investigations and corrections. Contact: Federal Services Bureau, 608-A Stonewall Lane, Fredericksburg, VA 22407.

■ **P.S.I.C.**

URL: N/A

A detailed job listing for entry level and lateral entry law enforcement career opportunities throughout the country, Contact P.S.I.C., P.O. Box 3831, Springfield, IL 62708.

■ **Tactical Advantage Press**

URL: N/A

The Law Enforcement Advisor—California Edition is a comprehensive guide for the 550 law enforcement agencies in California for job seekers for entry level positions. Contact: Tactical Advantage Press, P.O. Box 5652, Pasadena, CA 91107

■ **United States Law Enforcement Services**

URL: www.policecareers.com

A job seekers digest for federal agents, state troopers and sheriff deputies nationwide. Contact: U. S. Law Enforcement Service, P.O. Box 1322, Severna, MD 21146.

Your search for the hiring of law enforcement positions is not limited to merely the aforementioned sources. The success of your searching efforts is limited to only your imagination and persistence. There are any number of avenues in which to find agencies that are hiring. An important factor to keep in mind, however, is the essence of timing. You don't want to submit your application on the last date the recruitment is open. As noted in previous chapters, sometimes the date of the submission of application is ranked. If that occurs, you already are towards the bottom of the eligibility list. It takes time to fill out an application properly and to collate the necessary attachments. As you can see, there are clear benefits to timely notice. Following are a few more suggestions that may aid you in this regard.

Networking: You may have family members residing out of your immediate area. You may have made friends with co-workers who have moved out of state and established residency in an area that interests you for a career in law enforcement. These areas may very well not be represented on the various   means via the internet sources. The only way you will ever know if a law enforcement agency in these areas begins the recruitment process is if someone tells you. Call these family members, your former co-workers and your friends. Tell them about your ambitions and that you would like to be notified if and when a hiring process is advertised. Ask them to periodically check the classified ads in their local newspaper. People love to be of assistance, especially when they believe they are helping someone begin a new career. All agencies will hire eventually. It is inevitable.

Colleges: Colleges, especially junior colleges with a criminal justice, police science or law enforcement program, are an excellent resource for information of agencies intending to hire. There are two reasons for this. First, criminal justice departments tend to be on mailing lists for area law enforcement agencies. Junior colleges are often the resource sites for law ment in-service training programs and, as such, hiring brochures are regularly sent to them. Pay a visit to your local college and ask to view their bulletin board.

Secondly, most junior college criminal justice faculty is made up of part-time instructors. These part-time instructors are typically full-time law enforcement officials from surrounding communities. These instructors will most likely have knowledge about their own department's plans to hire, as well as other departments in the area.